EVOLVE

STUDENT'S BOOK

with Digital Pack

Ben Goldstein and Ceri Jones

6B

CAMBRIDGE
UNIVERSITY PRESS

Shaftesbury Road, Cambridge CB2 8EA, United Kingdom

One Liberty Plaza, 20th Floor, New York, NY 10006, USA

477 Williamstown Road, Port Melbourne, VIC 3207, Australia

314–321, 3rd Floor, Plot 3, Splendor Forum, Jasola District Centre, New Delhi – 110025, India

103 Penang Road, #05–06/07, Visioncrest Commercial, Singapore 238467

Cambridge University Press & Assessment is a department of the University of Cambridge.

It furthers the University's mission by disseminating knowledge in the pursuit of
education, learning and research at the highest international levels of excellence.

www.cambridge.org
Information on this title: www.cambridge.org/9781009237604

First published with Digital Pack 2022

20 19 18 17 16 15 14 13 12 11 10 9 8 7 6 5 4 3

Printed in Malaysia by Vivar Printing

A catalogue record for this publication is available from the British Library

ISBN 978-1-009-23088-9 Student's Book with eBook
ISBN 978-1-009-23758-1 Student's Book with Digital Pack
ISBN 978-1-009-23759-8 Student's Book with Digital Pack A
ISBN 978-1-009-23760-4 Student's Book with Digital Pack B
ISBN 978-1-108-40909-4 Workbook with Audio
ISBN 978-1-108-40885-1 Workbook with Audio A
ISBN 978-1-108-41196-7 Workbook with Audio B
ISBN 978-1-108-40520-1 Teacher's Edition with Test Generator
ISBN 978-1-108-41077-9 Presentation Plus
ISBN 978-1-108-41206-3 Class Audio CDs
ISBN 978-1-108-40802-8 Video Resource Book with DVD
ISBN 978-1-009-23070-4 Full Contact with Digital Pack

Additional resources for this publication at www.cambridge.org/evolve

ACKNOWLEDGMENTS

The *Evolve* publishers would like to thank the following individuals and institutions who have contributed their time and insights into the development of the course:

Antonio Machuca Montalvo, **Organización The Institute TITUELS**, Veracruz, Mexico; Asli Derin Anaç, **Istanbul Bilgi University**, Turkey; Claudia Piccoli Díaz **Harmon Hall**, Mexico; Professor Daniel Enrique Hernández Cruz, **Fundación Universitaria Unimonserrate**, Colombia; Daniel Martin, **CELLEP**, Brazil; Daniel Nowatnick, USA; Daniel Valderrama, **Centro Colombo Americano de Bogota**, Colombia; Diego Ribeiro Santos, **Universidade Anhembri Morumbi**, São Paulo, Brazil; Isabela Villas Boas, **Casa Thomas Jefferson**, Brasília, Brazil; Ivanova Monteros, **Universidad Tecnológica Equinoccial**, Ecuador; Lenise Butler, **Laureate Languages**, Mexico; Lillian Dantas; Professor Lizette Antonia Mendoza Huertas, **Fundación Universitaria Unimonserrate**, Colombia; Maria Araceli Hernández Tovar, **Instituto Tecnológico Superior de San Luis Potosí**, Capital, Mexico; Ray Purdey, **ELS Educational Services**; Roberta Freitas, **IBEU**, Rio de Janeiro, Brazil; Rosario Aste Rentería, **Instituto De Emprendedores USIL**, Peru; Verónica Nolivos Arellano, **Centro Ecuatoriano Norteamericano**, Quito, Equador.

To our speaking competition winners, who have contributed their ideas:

Ana Netto, Brazil; Andressa Zanfonatto Slongo, Brazil; Betsi García Alonso, Mexico; Carlos Alfredo Reyes, Honduras; Daniela Estefanía Mota Silva, Mexico; Katherine, Ecuador; Marcelo Piscitelli, Brazil; Renata Lima Cardoso Mendes, Brazil; Stephanie, Honduras; Victoria Rueda Leister Pinto, Brazil.

To our expert speakers, who have contributed their time:

Andrea Mendoza, Audrey Decker, Eric Rodriguez, João Glauber Barbosa, Ryoko Mathes, Susanne Gutermuth.

And special thanks to Wayne Rimmer for writing the Pronunciation sections, and to Laura Patsko for her expert input.

Authors' Acknowledgments

A special thanks to all the editorial team, particularly Dena Daniel, whose patience and professionalism helped make this project a pleasure to work on.

The authors and publishers acknowledge the following sources of copyright material and are grateful for the permissions granted. While every effort has been made, it has not always been possible to identify the sources of all the material used, or to trace all copyright holders. If any omissions are brought to our notice, we will be happy to include the appropriate acknowledgments on reprinting and in the next update to the digital edition, as applicable.

Key: REV = Review, U = Unit.

Text

U8: CNBC LLC. for the text from '6 tips for putting together the perfect elevator pitch' by Elizabeth Schulze, 05.12.2017. Copyright © CNBC LLC. Reproduced with permission; **U10**: Text about EXO. Copyright © EXO. Reproduced with kind permission; bio-bean Ltd for the text about 'bio-bean Ltd'. Reproduced with kind permission of Jessica Folkerts; **U12**: Michael Hauge for the article 'The Five Key Turning Points Of All Successful Movie Scripts' by Michael Hauge. Copyright © Michael Hauge. Reproduced with kind permission.

Photography

All photographs are sourced from Getty Images.

U7–U12: Tom Merton/Caiaimage; **U7**: valentinrussanov/E+; Inti St Clair; asiseeit/E+; Alfred Pasieka/Science Photo Library; Tek Image/Science Photo Library/Getty Images Plus; uschools/E+; rodho/iStock/Getty Images Plus; View Stock; Copyright Xinzheng. All Rights Reserved./Moment; Adriana O./Moment Open; kitamin/iStock/Getty Images Plus; Wibowo Rusli/Lonely Planet Images/Getty Images Plus; Pinghung Chen/EyeEm; Fernando Trabanco Fotografía/Moment; Manuel Breva Colmeiro/Moment; nrqemi/iStock/Getty Images Plus; FG Trade/E+; IgorKovalchuk/iStock/Getty Images Plus; ROMEO GACAD/AFP; Kylie McLaughlin/Lonely Planet Images/Getty Images Plus; **U8**: Dirk Anschutz/Stone/Getty Images Plus; Navaswan/Taxi/Getty Images Plus; Mike Harrington/Stone/Getty Images Plus; Punsayaporn Thaveekul/EyeEm; Tinpixels/E+; BanksPhotos/E+; Bertrand Demee/Photographer's Choice RF; **U9**: Artyom Geodakyan/TASS; Hero Images; Westend61; Caiaimage/Tom Merton; skynesher/E+; Cultura RM Exclusive/Frank and Helena/Getty Images Plus; westphalia/E+; Spondylolithesis/iStock/Getty Images Plus; RODGER BOSCH/AFP; Cultura Exclusive/WALTER ZERLA/Getty Images Plus; stevecoleimages/E+; Ariel Skelley/DigitalVision; Foodcollection GesmbH; filadendron/E+; Eva-Katalin/E+; mapodile/E+; Slavica/E+; Thomas Northcut/DigitalVision; Alfaproxima/iStock/Getty Images Plus;

U10: Fernando Trabanco Fotografía/Moment; Waitforlight/Moment Unreleased; Krit of Studio OMG/Moment; Kryssia Campos/Moment; grandriver/E+; Jef_M/iStock/Getty Images Plus; Juanmonino/E+; Thomas Imo/Photothek; Francesco Perre/EyeEm; Chee Siong Teh/EyeEm; Accessony/iStock/Getty Images Plus; Premyuda Yospim/iStock/Getty Images Plus; Tracy Packer Photography/Moment; andresr/E+; Michael Burrell/iStock/Getty Images Plus; Monika Ribbe/Photographer's Choice/Getty Images Plus; carlosalvarez/E+; Jutta Kuss; B&M Noskowski/E+; deimagine/E+; Tadamasa Taniguchi/Taxi/Getty Images Plus; DjelicS/E+; Chesnot/Getty Images News; **U11**: altrendo images/Juice Images; Andreas Korth/EyeEm; Abd Rahman Fahmi Mat Hasan/EyeEm; Tai Heng Leong/EyeEm; Neil Setchfield/Lonely Planet Images/Getty Images Plus; Andrey Nyrkov/EyeEm; quisp65/DigitalVision Vectors; Donato Sardella/Getty Images Entertainment; James Baigrie/Photodisc; photosindia; Elena_Danileiko/iStock/Getty Images Plus; Anikona/iStock/Getty Images Plus; NoirChocolate/iStock/Getty Images Plus; Clive Mason/Getty Images Sport; GREGG NEWTON/AFP; Icon Sportswire; John Russel/National Hockey League; BOLDG/iStock/Getty Images Plus; chelovek/iStock/Getty Images Plus; **U12**: DawidKasza/iStock/Getty Images Plus; Compassionate Eye Foundation/DigitalVision; sturti/E+; De Agostini/Archivio J. Lange/Getty Images Plus; Daniel Kreher; Anton Petrus/Moment; Bjorn Holland/Photodisc; by Edward Neyburg/Moment; Monica Rodriguez/The Image Bank/Getty Images Plus; Neil Mockford/GC Images; Barcroft Media; wabeno/iStock/Getty Images Plus; Car Culture; DNY59/E+; by wildestanimal/Moment; Colin Anderson Productions pty ltd/DigitalVision; vandervelden/E+; 3DMAVR/iStock/Getty Images Plus; **REV4**: Kikor.

The following photographs are sourced from other libraries/sources.

U9: Courtesy of LifeStraw; © Larry Fisher/Quad-City Times via ZUMA Wire; **U10**: © A photograph of Viva Technology 2018. Reproduced with kind permission of Stacey Binnion; © bio-bean Ltd.

Front cover photography by Hans Neleman/The Image Bank/Getty Images Plus/Getty Images.

Illustration

U9: Robert Filip (Good Illustration); **U11**: Ben Swift (NB Illustration); **U12**: 411 Jo (KJA Artists).

Audio production by CityVox, New York.

EVOLVE

SPEAKING MATTERS

EVOLVE is a six-level American English course for adults and young adults, taking students from beginner to advanced levels (CEFR A1 to C1).

Drawing on insights from language teaching experts and real students, EVOLVE is a general English course that gets students speaking with confidence.

This student-centered course covers all skills and focuses on the most effective and efficient ways to make progress in English.

Confidence in teaching.
Joy in learning.

Better Learning WITH EVOLVE

Better Learning is our simple approach where insights we've gained from research have helped shape content that drives results. Language evolves, and so does the way we learn. This course takes a flexible, student-centered approach to English language teaching.

EVOLVE
STUDENT'S BOOK
Ben Goldstein and Ceri Jones
6

Experience Better Learning

Meet our expert speakers

Our expert speakers are highly proficient non-native speakers of English living and working in the New York City area.

Videos and ideas from our expert speakers feature throughout the Student's Book for you to respond and react to.

Scan the QR codes below to listen to their stories.

Andrea Mendoza
from Colombia
Financial analyst

Eric Rodriguez
from Ecuador
Graphic designer

Ryoko Mathes
from Japan
Academic advisor

Audrey Decker
from France
Co-founder of a non-profit organization

João Glauber Barbosa
from Brazil
Works in finance for an insurance company.

Susanne Gutermuth
from Germany
Real estate agent

INSIGHT

Research shows that achievable speaking role models can be a powerful motivator.

CONTENT

Bite-sized videos feature expert speakers talking about topics in the Student's Book.

RESULT

Students are motivated to speak and share their ideas.

Student-generated content

EVOLVE is the first course of its kind to feature real student-generated content. We spoke to more than 2,000 students from all over the world about the topics they would like to discuss in English and in what situations they would like to be able to speak more confidently. Their ideas are included throughout the Student's Book.

"It's important to provide learners with interesting or stimulating topics."

Teacher, Mexico (Global Teacher Survey, 2017)

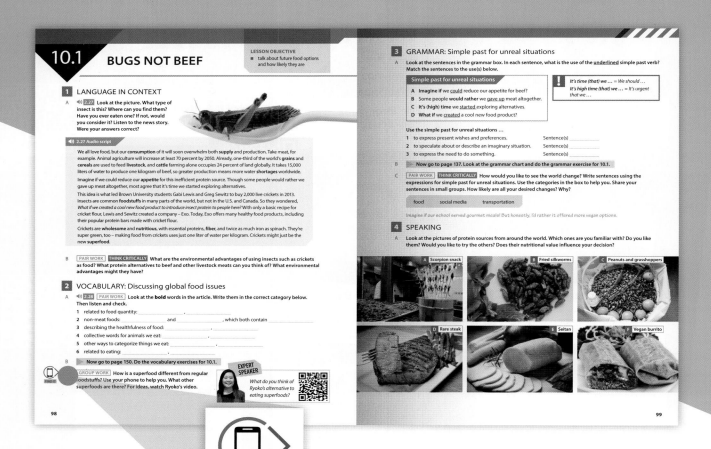

Find it

FIND IT

INSIGHT

Research with hundreds of teachers and students across the globe revealed a desire to expand the classroom and bring the real world in.

CONTENT

Find it are smartphone activities that allow students to bring live content into the class and personalize the learning experience with research and group activities.

RESULT

Students engage in the lesson because it is meaningful to them.

Designed for success

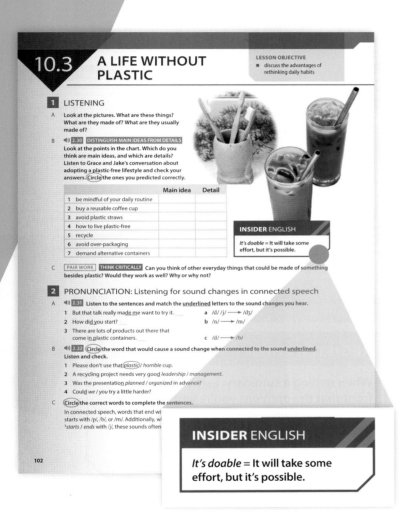

Pronunciation

INSIGHT

Research shows that only certain aspects of pronunciation actually affect comprehensibility and inhibit communication.

CONTENT

EVOLVE focuses on the aspects of pronunciation that most affect communication.

RESULT

Students understand more when listening and can be clearly understood when they speak.

Insider English

INSIGHT

Even in a short exchange, idiomatic language can inhibit understanding.

CONTENT

Insider English focuses on the informal language and colloquial expressions frequently found in everyday situations.

RESULT

Students are confident in the real world.

10.4 WHAT'S YOURS IS MINE

LESSON OBJECTIVE
- write a summary of a discussion about the new economy

1 READING

A Look at the picture of people using a ride-share service. Is this an example of the *gig economy* or the *sharing economy*? What's the difference? You can use your phone to help you. What's your opinion of these new economic models? Why?

B PREDICT CONTENT Look at the key words related to the discussion thread below. Which do you think will be used to defend new economic models and which to criticize them? Read the thread and check your answers.

| unfair competition | human-scale commerce | minimum wage |

THE NEW ECONOMY: HAVE YOUR SAY!

Who are the real winners and losers in the gig economy? Is a sharing economy model any better? What do you think?

A Kevin
When you read about the gig economy, it seems great for everybody, but let me tell you, there are losers in this story. Like taxi drivers. In some countries, it's very expensive to obtain a license – it's an investment. And once you get one, that's your job for life. Then ride-share companies come along, and because of the increased competition, they take away the taxi drivers' livelihood. It's unfair competition because it doesn't cost the other drivers much at all.

B Amanda
It's time that an economy based on everyone having regular, long-term jobs was challenged. The gig economy is all about on-demand services. Conditions might be more precarious for the worker – job security, insurance, benefits, etc., but we have to get used to that. It's the way the world is going.

C Abdul
What I like about the sharing economy is that it's a human-scale version of commerce, where you often meet the person who you're doing business with. Take Airbnb. That's a whole lot better than staying in an anonymous hotel somewhere. It's much more personal, and you get better service because of it.

D Daniel
The sharing economy is nothing new. Just look at libraries. We're just extending that model into the high-tech world. It's inevitable, like economic evolution. There's nothing we can do to stop it, so we might as well go with it.

E Laura
The "gig economy" business model revolves around tech companies that view legal regulations as outdated or irrelevant. They don't want to follow the rules, so they come up with a way to get around them. They still make money, but the people actually doing the work are NOT better off. In fact, the workers are all independent contractors rather than employees, so they don't get vacations or a minimum wage or sick pay or help saving for retirement. And what's worse, they can be fired without warning or explanation, so they can't even complain!

F Carolina
At first glance, I really liked the idea of opening up the economy. It's great for us customers, but I think a lot of people actually lose out. I mean, look at streaming music services. We save by not having to download music, but how much money do the musicians make once all the middlemen take their cut? And the food delivery apps! They take such a large cut that many restaurants can't afford to use them, so they lose customers they used to have. People need to understand that these cool new companies could be destroying small neighborhood businesses.

G Sven
Not so fast! In many places the gig economy has really benefited people, like places where there are no taxis, for example. Now people can use a ride service. How is that a bad thing? People can make extra money and learn new skills. I read that Uber offers English courses to their drivers because they know that it'll help them in their work.

C PAIR WORK EVALUATE INFORMATION Put a check (✓) for the contributors in favor of the new economic models and an X (✗) for those against them. Highlight the main idea in each comment.

D GROUP WORK THINK CRITICALLY Which of the opinions in the discussion thread do you agree with? Why? What could be the long-term effects of these new economic models?

104

2 WRITING

A Read the summary of the discussion thread. Does it focus on arguments for or against new economic models?

The gig economy and sharing economy raise many different issues and opinions. The topic is **not at all** a simple one, but two clear arguments in favor of new economic models emerge from the discussion thread: freedom of choice and flexibility.

Gig and sharing economy practices liberate people from the rigidity of a traditional working model, **so** it is beneficial to society. **In terms of** customers, they can have whatever they want when they want it – music, a place to stay, food delivery, a ride to the airport. **And for** workers, they are their own bosses, free to set their own hours and determine their income by working as much as they want. **In a nutshell**, the freedom and flexibility offered by these new ways of working make it beneficial to everyone.

Though **probably true** that the gig/sharing economy is here to stay, **even if** we don't like it, the freedom and flexibility it offers has won it many champions.

B USE APPROPRIATE REGISTER Look at the **bold** expressions in the summary and their synonyms in the box below. Which set is more formal? Which expressions from the box could substitute for each expression in the summary?

by no means	in brief	in this respect
it would seem	regarding	regardless of whether
with respect to		

WRITE IT

C PLAN You're going to write a formal summary of the negative viewpoints expressed in the discussion thread. With a partner, look at the main ideas you identified in exercise 1C. What themes could you focus on in your summary?

D PAIR WORK Examine the structure of the summary of positive viewpoints in exercise 2A and discuss the questions.
- What is the role of each paragraph?
- How many points are presented in the body (middle) paragraph?

E PAIR WORK Work together to write your summary in 150–200 words. Use formal expressions like those in exercise 2B.

F GROUP WORK Share your summary with another pair of students and offer feedback. Is the register definitely more formal than the comments in the thread? Did they present all the main points? Did you organize your summaries around the same or different themes?

105

REGISTER CHECK

When writing a summary, establish up front that the opinions you're writing about are not your own and then write from that perspective. This avoids the constant repetition of phrases like *According to …* and *As stated by …* .

Register check

INSIGHT
Teachers report that their students often struggle to master the differences between written and spoken English.

CONTENT
Register check draws on research into the Cambridge English Corpus and highlights potential problem areas for learners.

RESULT
Students transition confidently between written and spoken English and recognize different levels of formality as well as when to use them appropriately.

> "The presentation is very clear, and there are plenty of opportunities for student practice and production."

Jason Williams, Teacher, Notre Dame Seishin University, Japan

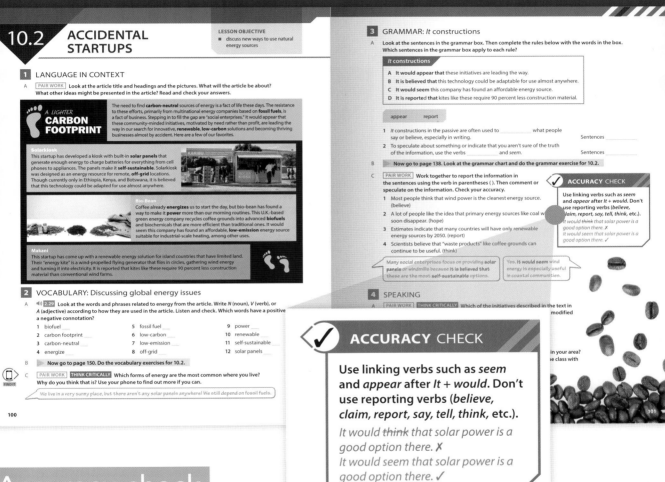

Accuracy check

INSIGHT
Some common errors can become fossilized if not addressed early on in the learning process.

CONTENT
Accuracy check highlights common learner errors (based on unique research into the Cambridge Learner Corpus) and can be used for self-editing.

RESULT
Students avoid common errors in their written and spoken English.

You spoke. We listened.

Students told us that speaking is the most important skill for them to master, while teachers told us that finding speaking activities that engage their students and work in the classroom can be challenging.

That's why EVOLVE has a whole lesson dedicated to speaking: Lesson 5, *Time to speak*.

Time to speak

INSIGHT

Speaking ability is how students most commonly measure their own progress but is also the area where they feel most insecure. To be able to fully exploit speaking opportunities in the classroom, students need a safe speaking environment where they can feel confident, supported, and able to experiment with language.

CONTENT

Time to speak is a unique lesson dedicated to developing speaking skills and is based around immersive tasks that involve information sharing and decision making.

RESULT

Time to speak lessons create a buzz in the classroom where speaking can really thrive, evolve, and take off, resulting in more confident speakers of English.

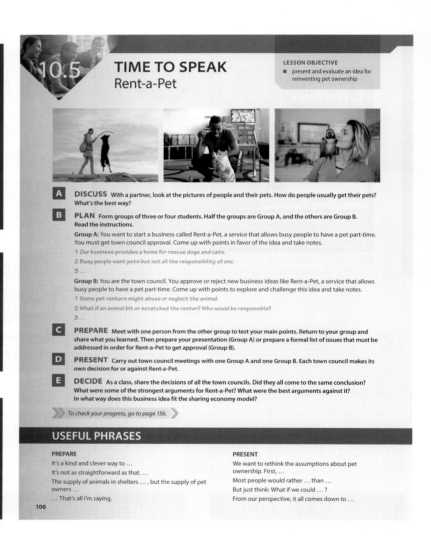

10.5

TIME TO SPEAK
Rent-a-Pet

LESSON OBJECTIVE
■ present and evaluate an idea for reinventing pet ownership

A   **DISCUSS**   With a partner, look at the pictures of people and their pets. How do people usually get their pets? What's the best way?

B   **PLAN**   Form groups of three or four students. Half the groups are Group A, and the others are Group B. Read the instructions.

Group A: You want to start a business called Rent-a-Pet, a service that allows busy people to have a pet part-time. You must get town council approval. Come up with points in favor of the idea and take notes.
1 Our business provides a home for rescue dogs and cats.
2 Busy people want pets but not all the responsibility of one.
3 …

Group B: You are the town council. You approve or reject new business ideas like Rent-a-Pet, a service that allows busy people to have a pet part-time. Come up with points to explore and challenge this idea and take notes.
1 Some pet renters might abuse or neglect the animal.
2 What if an animal bit or scratched the renter? Who would be responsible?
3 …

C   **PREPARE**   Meet with one person from the other group to test your main points. Return to your group and share what you learned. Then prepare your presentation (Group A) or prepare a formal list of issues that must be addressed in order for Rent-a-Pet to get approval (Group B).

D   **PRESENT**   Carry out town council meetings with one Group A and one Group B. Each town council makes its own decision for or against Rent-a-Pet.

E   **DECIDE**   As a class, share the decisions of all the town councils. Did they all come to the same conclusion? What were some of the strongest arguments for Rent-a-Pet? What were the best arguments against it? In what way does this business idea fit the sharing economy model?

⟩⟩ To check your progress, go to page 156. ⟩

USEFUL PHRASES

PREPARE
It's a kind and clever way to …
It's not as straightforward as that. …
The supply of animals in shelters … , but the supply of pet owners …
… That's all I'm saying.

PRESENT
We want to rethink the assumptions about pet ownership. First, …
Most people would rather … than …
But just think: What if we could … ?
From our perspective, it all comes down to …

106

Experience Better Learning with EVOLVE: a course that helps both teachers and students on every step of the language learning journey.

Speaking matters. Find out more about creating safe speaking environments in the classroom.

EVOLVE unit structure

Unit opening page

Each unit opening page activates prior knowledge and vocabulary and immediately gets students speaking.

Lessons 1 and 2

These lessons present and practice the unit vocabulary and grammar in context, helping students discover language rules for themselves. Students then have the opportunity to use this language in well-scaffolded, personalized speaking tasks.

Lesson 3

This lesson is built around an off-the-page dialogue that practices listening skills. It also models and contextualizes useful speaking skills. The final speaking task draws on the language and strategies from the lesson.

Lesson 4

This is a skills lesson based around an engaging reading. Each lesson asks students to think critically and ends with a practical writing task.

Lesson 5

Time to speak is an entire lesson dedicated to developing speaking skills. Students work on collaborative, immersive tasks, which involve information sharing and decision making.

CONTENTS

Listening	Speaking skills	Reading	Writing	Speaking
The story of a returnee ■ An interview with someone who has just returned from her ancestral home	■ Comment on your own story ■ Express an opinion ■ Respond to someone else's story	**When a language dies** ■ A graph and text about languages in danger of extinction	**Summary of a story** ■ Parallel structures	■ Discuss the pros and cons of DNA tests ■ Talk about the occasions that bring your family together ■ Tell stories about visiting new places ■ Synthesize the main points in a story **Time to speak** ■ Discuss a local festivity and decide the best way to promote it
It's the app you need ■ A conversation between an app designer and a friend	■ Speak persuasively about a product	**The perfect pitch** ■ An article about developing a pitch for investors	**Presentation slides** ■ Presentation formats	■ Talk about the distractions in your life ■ Talk about how important instinct is in daily life ■ Discuss the apps that make your life easier ■ Compare presentation slides **Time to speak** ■ Present a pitch to investors for an idea or product
Clearing the air ■ An interview with a politician about clean air issues	■ Ask probing questions ■ Buy time to think / deflect questions	**A thirsty world** ■ Three short articles about water crises around the world and water charities that address them	**A short article** ■ Phrases to highlight viewpoint	■ Talk about ways to discourage a sedentary lifestyle ■ Discuss a sleep plan for different people ■ Discuss important local issues in a role-play activity ■ Consider strengths and weaknesses of an initiative **Time to speak** ■ Present choices for other people based on their priorities
A life without plastic ■ A conversation about the challenges and value of going plastic-free	■ Defend an opinion ■ Conclude a turn	**What's yours is mine** ■ Short texts from a forum about new economic models	**A summary of a discussion** ■ Avoiding opinion in a summary ■ Marking opinion in a summary	■ Discuss alternative food options ■ Discuss renewable energy ■ Debate alternative lifestyle choices that benefit the environment ■ Consider the conclusions from a discussion **Time to speak** ■ Debate the pros and cons of a local initiative
It tastes like green! ■ A Q&A session with two experts on the psychology of color	■ Respond to questions for different purposes	**A sense of identity** ■ An article on the significance of colors in sports marketing	**An opinion essay** ■ Express and support opinions with examples	■ Discuss the best color scheme for different products and companies ■ Discuss color expressions ■ Consider what effect color has on taste expectations ■ Discuss the arguments presented by others and offer feedback for improvement **Time to speak** ■ Discuss and present the characteristics that define a group's identity
"And that's when it all changed!" ■ A story about a celebrity impersonator	■ Retell a story ■ Refer to the original story ■ Skip details	**"The next thing you know, …"** ■ An article about the structure of a successful movie script	**Movie review** ■ Write concise descriptions (multi-clause sentences)	■ Practice giving job interview answers ■ Talk about how things have changed dramatically ■ Retell a story ■ Describe plots and turning points **Time to speak** ■ Develop a creative story based on pictures

This page is intentionally left blank

UNIT OBJECTIVES
- discuss the growing interest in DNA testing and genealogy
- talk about celebrations in your family and community
- share a story about visiting a place with special significance
- summarize information about a topic
- present a plan to promote a cultural celebration

ROOTS

7

START SPEAKING

A Look at the picture. How are the people probably related? Which of your relatives are you most similar to physically? Are you similar in other ways, too (style, personality, gestures, etc.)?

B How many generations of your family have you met? How much family history do you know? What or who would you like to know more about? Why?

C Does everyone in your family come from the same area? If not, where do (or did) they come from? Where do they live now? For ideas, watch Andrea's video.

EXPERT SPEAKER

How is your family similar to Andrea's?

IT'S IN THE BLOOD

1 LANGUAGE IN CONTEXT

A **What does the graphic show? Why do you think people want to know information like this? Would you like to have your DNA tested? Why or why not?**

B **Read the article. Whose results are shown in the pie chart above? Why did the two people decide to take the test? How do they each feel about their results? What do you think your reaction would be?**

DNA Results

- **52%** Southern Europe
- **21%** Southeast Asia
- **15%** Native American
- **2%** Neanderthal
- **10%** Other regions

! *DNA* = deoxyribonucleic acid, a chemical in the cells of living things that contains genetic information

What's so great about your DNA?

DNA **ancestry** kits are all the rage these days, with companies in fierce competition to provide the cheapest, most accurate, most detailed information about a person's **genetic** history. But what do people really gain from this information?

CRISTIANO | 40, Texas

My wife gave me the kit as a birthday present. No way would I have done it otherwise. I already knew a lot about my family's **heritage**, so I sent off my sample for testing and forgot about it. Little did I know how fascinating my results would be! My father's family goes back to Italy, and my mother's family has Native American roots, but never had I imagined that I had **ancestors** from Asia, nor that I'm 2% Neanderthal! Now I'm hooked on **genealogy** – and my wife wishes she'd bought me a tie.

SABINE | 22, Quebec

I was adopted as a baby, and we only have a little information about my birth mother. I thought the DNA test might help answer some questions. My dark skin comes from my mother, but who did I **inherit** these green eyes from? I was excited to learn more, but only when the results arrived did I realize how little my **ethnic** background really matters. Not until then did I fully appreciate my wonderful **adoptive** parents. I can now say that my background is mainly Afro-Caribbean with a touch of French, but so what? I am who I am because of my upbringing. That's far more important than genes.

INSIDER ENGLISH

a touch of = a small amount of

2 VOCABULARY: Talking about ancestry

A 🔊 **2.02** Use the **bold** words in the article to complete the word families. Then listen to check your work.

Abstract nouns	Nouns	Verbs	Adjectives
adoption		adopt	*adoptive* / adopted
			ancestral
ethnicity			
	genes		
			hereditary

B ▶ **Now go to page 147. Do the vocabulary exercises for 7.1.**

C PAIR WORK THINK CRITICALLY **Which do you think has a greater influence on who a person is, upbringing or genes? Why? What examples can you think of to support your ideas?**

3 GRAMMAR: Negative and limiting adverbials

A **Read the sentences in the grammar box. Complete the rules.**

> ### Negative and limiting adverbials
>
> **No way** would I have done it otherwise.
>
> **Little** did I know how fascinating my results would be!
>
> **Never** had I imagined that I had ancestors from Asia.
>
> **Only when the results arrived** did I realize how little my ethnic background matters.
>
> **Not until then** did I fully appreciate my wonderful adoptive parents.

To add emphasis, you can start a sentence with a negative or limiting adverbial phrase.

1 Examples of negative adverbials include *No way*, *Never*, and _____ .

2 Examples of limiting adverbials include _____ *did* … and *Only when* ….

3 When a sentence starts with a negative or limiting adverbial phrase, the word order in the verb phrase changes so that the auxiliary verb for that tense comes before the _____ .

4 When the verb is simple present or simple past, it expands to include the auxiliary verb *do/does* or _____ .

B ▶ **Now go to page 134. Look at the grammar chart and do the grammar exercise for 7.1.**

C PAIR WORK **Find and correct the mistakes in the sentences. Check your accuracy. What additional uses of the information from DNA tests does each sentence describe? Discuss with a partner.**

1 Not only you can find out about your ancestors, you can also learn about possible hereditary health influences.

2 Only when you subscribe you get a full report about possible previously unknown relatives.

3 Little realize people that they're giving away their full genetic code, which might be shared with other organizations.

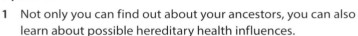

> ✓ **ACCURACY** CHECK
>
> **When the verb is in the simple present, remember to include *do/does*.**
>
> *Little* ~~they know~~ *what awaits them.* ✗
> *Little do they know what awaits them.* ✓

4 SPEAKING

A GROUP WORK THINK CRITICALLY **What might be some of the disadvantages of having your DNA tested? Make a list of questions to ask a DNA testing service.**

B **Share your questions with the class and discuss them.**

> We wondered about privacy. Can anybody see my **genetic** information? I mean, **no way would I want** total strangers to have detailed information about my **ethnic heritage**!

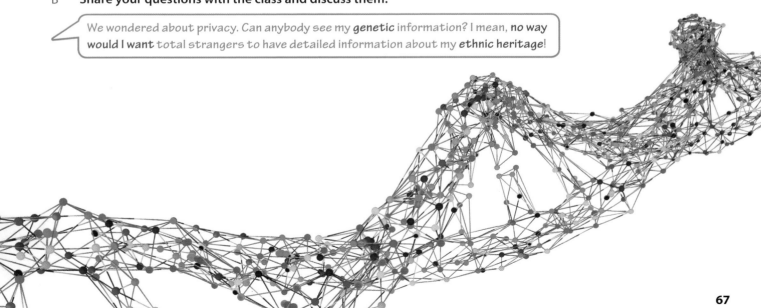

7.2 | A VERY SPECIAL OCCASION

LESSON OBJECTIVE
- talk about celebrations in your family and community

1 LANGUAGE IN CONTEXT

A 🔊 **2.03** **Look at the pictures. What celebration do these things relate to? What culture uses them? Listen to part of a podcast to check your answers. Does the speaker enjoy this occasion?**

> 🔊 **2.03 Audio script**
>
> On the table sits an enormous bowl of oranges and tangerines – they **symbolize** wealth. Around the walls hang red and gold decorations – they **signify** good luck. And through the kitchen door wafts the delicious smell of fresh dumplings. It's Chinese New Year, and we're all at my grandmother's house to **mark** the occasion and take part in the **festivities**.
>
> My grandmother's been preparing for this moment for days. First, she cleaned the house from top to bottom. This **ritual** sweeps away past bad luck. Then she decorated with lanterns and banners that wish everyone good fortune and good health!
>
> Everywhere I look I see red – the main color for any Chinese celebration because it's supposed to bring good luck. On the red tablecloth in the dining room lies a stack of red envelopes. In the envelopes are crisp new dollar bills. The older generations give these to the younger members of the family. This **practice** has a special **significance**, reminding the younger generation of the debt they owe their elders.
>
> My grandmother came to the United States as a child, but she works hard to **keep our traditions alive**. That's why it's so important that we're all here today to **observe** the ancient **rites**, to **honor** our grandmother and heritage, and to **pay tribute to** all our ancestors.

B 🔊 **2.03** **PAIR WORK** **Listen again and read. In the speaker's culture, what's the significance of cleaning the house? The color red? The envelopes of money? What are some things associated with a celebration that you enjoy?**

INSIDER ENGLISH

from top to bottom = **very thoroughly**

2 VOCABULARY: Talking about customs and traditions

A 🔊 **2.04** **PAIR WORK** **Look at the bold words in the script and use them to answer the questions below. Listen and check. Can you think of an example from your life or family for each answer?**

1 Which verbs match these objects? (More than one correct answer is possible.)

    a <u>mark, observe</u> an occasion   **c** _____ older relatives and ancestors

    b _____ good luck or good health   **d** _____ family traditions

2 Which nouns apply to these meanings? (More than one correct answer is possible.)

    a types of customs: _____

    b all the things done as part of a celebration: _____

    c a special meaning attached to an action or object: _____

B ▶ **Now go to page 147. Do the vocabulary exercises for 7.2.**

C **PAIR WORK** **THINK CRITICALLY** **Why do you think the speaker's grandmother gives so much significance to marking this occasion? Why might it have been difficult for her to keep the tradition alive?**

3 GRAMMAR: Fronting adverbials

A **Read the sentences in the grammar box. Then complete the rules below.**

> **Fronting adverbials**
>
> **Through the kitchen door** wafts the delicious smell of fresh dumplings.
> **On the red tablecloth** lies a stack of red envelopes.
> **In the envelopes** are crisp new dollar bills.

1 To add dramatic effect, you can bring adverbials of place or movement to **the front** / **the end** of a sentence.
2 The subject and verb of the main clause change position when …
   ■ the verb is *be*.
   ■ the verb indicates placement, like *sit* or _____ .
   ■ the verb indicates movement, like *fly* or _____ .

B ➤ **Now go to page 134. Look at the grammar chart and do the grammar exercise for 7.2.**

C PAIR WORK **Add dramatic effect by bringing the adverbials in bold to the front of the sentence. Make any changes to word order that are needed, and check your accuracy. What occasion do you think is being described?**

1 Sounds of laughter and scents of cooking come **from the kitchen**.
2 A huge turkey sits **in the oven** slowly roasting.
3 Three generations of the family wait **in the dining room**, ready to eat!
4 We hear the distant sounds of a football game **from the TV in the living room**.

✓ **ACCURACY** CHECK

In a sentence with a <u>direct object</u>, such as *We found <u>family portraits</u> in the library*, the word order does NOT change when there is a fronting adverbial.

In the library ~~found we~~ family portraits. ✗
In the library we found family portraits. ✓

4 SPEAKING

A GROUP WORK THINK CRITICALLY **Discuss the questions.**

   ■ What rites usually bring your family members together, even those who live far away?
   ■ Why do people make so much effort to observe rites, rituals, and customs? What significance do they hold?
   ■ What rituals does your family observe around specific occasions? Do you have any rituals that are unique to your family? What are they?

> In my family, we **mark** every birthday with a party. My mom decorates the whole house, and it's beautiful!

B **Do you enjoy big family get-togethers? Why or why not? For ideas, watch Andrea's video.**

EXPERT SPEAKER

Why do you think Andrea mentions her children?

THE STORY OF A RETURNEE

1 LISTENING

A 🔊 **2.05** Look at the pictures from Katerina's trip. Where do you think she went? Why do you think she went there? Listen to Katerina being interviewed about the trip. Were you right?

B 🔊 **2.05** **PAIR WORK** **LISTEN FOR ATTITUDE** How did the following things affect Katerina? How does she feel looking back on the experience? How do you know? Discuss your ideas with a partner. Listen again to check your answers.

■ the way it looked ■ meeting her relatives ■ the food

FIND IT

C 🔊 **2.05** **PAIR WORK** **DEDUCE MEANING** What do you think these words and phrases from the interview mean? Listen again and use the context to help you figure them out. Write your definitions. Then use a dictionary or your phone to check your answers.

1 You can say that again! _____
2 idyllic: _____
3 harbor: _____
4 exhausting: _____
5 frantically: _____
6 a stone's throw: _____

D **GROUP WORK** **THINK CRITICALLY** Join another pair of students and discuss the questions.

■ Do you know anyone like Katerina, who has roots in more than one culture? How did they end up where they are? Do they still have relatives in the other culture(s)? Do they ever visit them there?

■ What are some of the advantages and disadvantages of coming from a bicultural background?

2 PRONUNCIATION: Listening for missing /t/ and /d/ sounds

A 🔊 **2.06** **PAIR WORK** Listen to the sentences. Which of the underlined /t/ and /d/ sounds are pronounced? Circle them. Compare with a partner.

1 I have to admit, it's a little weird, as well. It's difficult to put into words.
2 Especially visiting my grandparents' village. I mean, they told me so many stories about this village that I'd built this kind of idyllic picture of it in my mind.

B 🔊 **2.07** **PAIR WORK** Listen to the sentences. Which of the underlined /t/ and /d/ sounds are **not** pronounced? Cross them out. Compare with a partner.

1 Sounds intriguing. Tell us about seeing the place for the first time, your first impressions.
2 I think I can understand that. And did you meet your cousins that day?
3 That was the best part! It was like being back in my grandmother's kitchen.
4 The food and the setting just went together.

C Circle the correct words to complete the sentence.

When /t/ and /d/ sounds come ¹*in the middle / at the end* of three consonants, ²*except for / including* between words, they are often left out.

3 SPEAKING SKILLS

A **PAIR WORK** Read the expressions in the chart aloud. How do the expressions within each set relate to each other? Match each set to a heading in the box and write it in.

| Commenting on your own story | Expressing an opinion | Responding to someone else's story |

I have to admit, …. To tell you the truth, … To be (perfectly) honest, … Don't get me wrong, …	I can see how it would be strange. I think I can understand that. How did you handle that? It must have been pretty overwhelming. It can't have been easy.	It's difficult to put into words. It's hard to describe. It's difficult to say why exactly. That was the best part! … if you know what I mean.

B **PAIR WORK** Think of a personal story about one of the topics below. Use phrases from the chart above as you tell your partner the story. Respond to your partner's story as you listen.

The first time you were the center of attention at an event

The first time you met someone in person that you had heard or read a lot about

4 PRONUNCIATION: Saying diphthongs

A 🔊 **2.08** Listen for the diphthongs in each word. How many sounds do you hear for each one?

/eɪ/ str<u>a</u>nge   /aɪ/ descr<u>i</u>be   /ɔɪ/ disapp<u>oi</u>ntment   /oʊ/ <u>o</u>verwhelming   /aʊ/ backgr<u>ou</u>nd

B 🔊 **2.09** **PAIR WORK** Unscramble the sounds into words and ⃝circle the diphthongs. Listen and check. Then work with a partner and use the sounds to make at least one other word with the same diphthong.

1 en / ʃən / dʒ / ə / r / eɪ   dʒenəreɪʃən – generation   /reɪdʒ/ – rage
2 tɪn / aʊ / n / m   _____   _____
3 aɪ / s / ə / ţ / iː / s / ə   _____   _____
4 m / ɪ / əʳ / p / l / ɔɪ / r   _____   _____
5 p / n / v / g / r / eɪ / aɪ   _____   _____
6 g / b / æ / d / k / aʊ / n / r   _____   _____
7 eɪ / f / ɪ / æ / ŋ / sɪn / t   _____   _____
8 r / b / əʳ / ɑː / k / oʊ / t   _____   _____

C **PAIR WORK** Write the new words you made above on a separate piece of paper, but scramble the sounds. Give your list to another pair of students. Can they figure out your words?

5 SPEAKING

A **Think about a time when you visited a place that holds significance for your family or met relatives for the first time.**

■ What things felt familiar? What things felt strange?

■ Were you disappointed, or did reality exceed your expectations? Why?

B **GROUP WORK** Tell your stories and comment as you listen.

> They kept asking me if I remembered all these people and places. I didn't want to be rude, but to be honest, I didn't remember anything!

> I can see how that would be awkward.

WHEN A LANGUAGE DIES

1 READING

A Look at the graph. What does it tell us about world languages? What information do you find the most interesting or surprising?

B READ FOR MAIN IDEAS Read the three texts below. Match them to the correct main ideas.

a Minority languages should be saved. ____

b Minority languages should be allowed to die out. ____

c The story of a minority language ____

Write an appropriate title for each text based on its main idea.

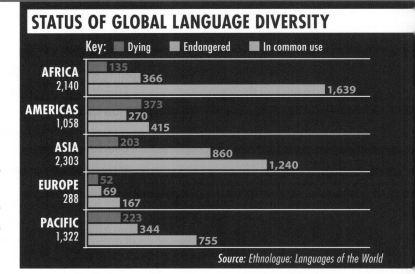

STATUS OF GLOBAL LANGUAGE DIVERSITY

Key: ■ Dying ■ Endangered ■ In common use

AFRICA 2,140 — 135 / 366 / 1,639

AMERICAS 1,058 — 373 / 270 / 415

ASIA 2,303 — 203 / 860 / 1,240

EUROPE 288 — 52 / 69 / 167

PACIFIC 1,322 — 223 / 344 / 755

Source: Ethnologue: Languages of the World

1 _____

A few years ago a compelling story was circulating on the internet. The last two speakers of the language Ayapaneco didn't like each other and had refused to talk to each other for decades. This ancient language was destined to die out, all because of the stubbornness of two old men!

Social media fanned the flames of the story, and it went viral – even taken up as part of an advertising campaign for a phone company. But of course, the story was too good to be true. Yes, their language was in danger, but they were not the only people who spoke it. And though the two men weren't the best of friends, neither were they giving each other the silent treatment.

Though the story may be false, the true tale is still worth telling. The two old men, along with other members of their family and community, were giving language lessons to the children in the village. The number of speakers had more than doubled in a few years. Far from losing their linguistic heritage, they had actually managed to save it!

Source: Schwa Fire

2 _____

There are about 7,000 living languages spoken around the world today. That might seem like a lot, but the number is diminishing. Experts estimate that we now lose a language every two weeks. Many scholars predict that by the end of the 21st century, we will have lost 50–90 percent of all languages spoken today. And each time we lose a language, our collective knowledge of the human experience is reduced.

A language is so much more than a channel for communication. It is the reflection of a unique interpretation of the world. This is especially true of oral languages. Of the 2,400 languages that researchers estimate are in immediate danger of extinction, many have no written form. All the wisdom and knowledge conveyed by those languages is passed from generation to generation through speaking. When the last speakers die, that wisdom dies with them.

Sources: Ethnologue, Day Translations, Pendleton Translations

3 _____

Linguistic landscapes are like ecosystems: They grow and adapt based on need and usage. Some languages blossom and grow; others wither away and die. It's nature's way. As much as I sympathize with speakers of minority languages who are fighting to keep their languages alive, sometimes extinction is inevitable. And when a language ceases to serve the needs of the community, hanging on only in the nostalgic conversations of village elders, then its time has come. The most gracious thing to do at that point is let it die, gently and peacefully.

Rather than desperately striving to breathe life back into dying languages, let us instead honor them by collecting written records, compiling dictionaries, forming academic societies to preserve their history. These are all valid linguistic pursuits that pay tribute to a lost culture but also let it die with dignity.

C PAIR WORK READ FOR ATTITUDE Read the three texts again. Which writer is the most emotionally engaged? Why do you think so?

D GROUP WORK THINK CRITICALLY What are some possible advantages of speaking a minority language? What actions could people take to try to save a language from extinction? Do you think these efforts should be made? Why or why not?

2 WRITING

A   **Read the summary of the three texts from exercise 1B. Has the writer fairly captured the main ideas and arguments of all three? Is any key information missing? Does the summary draw on one of the stories more than the others?**

Human-interest stories like the one about the two feuding old men who refused to speak to each other in their dying language draw attention to the issue of minority languages around the world, but they tend to oversimplify the situation. The question of how to save these languages, and whether it's actually worth reviving them, is a complex one. **On one side**, linguists argue that each language embodies a unique view of the world, thus should be saved, **while on the other**, pragmatists point out that when a language dies, it may well be because it is no longer relevant in the world, so its death is natural and should be accepted as such.

B   **SUMMARIZE ARGUMENTS** **Look at the bold phrases in the essay above. How do they relate to each other? Rewrite the end of the essay using one of the other parallel structures below.**

Some argue that … but others disagree, saying …

While some say … , others feel …

Many claim that … However, others maintain that …

WRITE IT

C   ▶   GROUP WORK   **Student A: Go to page 157. Student B: Go to page 158. Student C: Go to page 159. Follow the instructions.**

D   **PLAN** **You're going to write a paragraph summarizing the main arguments around the value of writing by hand in 100–120 words. Use your notes from exercise 2C and share the key points with your partners. Take notes on the information they share. Review the model paragraph above for structure.**

E   **Write your paragraph, drawing on information in all three texts. Present different perspectives by using parallel structures.**

F   GROUP WORK   **With the same two partners, read your paragraphs. Did you all include the same key points? Do you detect any bias or personal opinion in their paragraphs?**

TIME TO SPEAK
Preserving a custom

FIND IT

A **DISCUSS** Look at the pictures of Songkran festivities. In small groups, talk about what the people are doing. Where do you think these festivities take place? What might this practice symbolize? Use your phone to go online and learn about it.

B Think of a special occasion or cultural celebration that you know well. Share your personal experiences of it. Recall as many details as possible about its traditions and origins.

FIND IT

C **PREPARE** As a group, choose one of the events you discussed. Put together a plan to promote it on social media and in your community. Try to appeal to people who may not know about it. Choose one or more of the promotional tools from the box. What other tools should you consider? Why? You can look online to get ideas.

competitions	flyers and posters	local celebrity endorsements
local TV and radio spots	social media posts	

D **PRESENT** Divide your plan into sections, one per person in your group, and decide which person will present each part. Practice your part of the presentation within your group. Then present your whole plan to the class.

E **AGREE** As a class, discuss which plans were the most interesting. Which do you think will be most effective? Which event would you personally most like to attend? Why?

>> *To check your progress, go to page 155.*

USEFUL PHRASES

DISCUSS

The thing that makes it special for me is …

From every direction come the sounds of …

Not until you take part it in yourself do you fully appreciate the …

PRESENT

In the center of the poster sits a colorful …

It's really important to stress that it's fun for the whole family …

UNIT OBJECTIVES

- discuss distractions and attention spans
- talk about instincts and gut reactions
- describe the best features and selling points of apps
- write presentation slides
- pitch a company, an idea, or a product to investors

START SPEAKING

A   Look at the picture. What do you think is happening? Are all the kids engaged with it? How can you tell? Can you find one child who is not engaged with the activitiy? How can you tell?

B   How long can you stay focused on an activity if it's something you want to do? How about if you don't want to do it? Think of some examples for both scenarios.

C   What techniques do you use to stay focused on a task? Do you know of any others? For ideas, watch Eric's video.

EXPERT SPEAKER

What do you think of Eric's techniques?

8.1 THE ATTENTION SPAN MYTH

1 LANGUAGE IN CONTEXT

A 🔊 **2.10** **Look at the picture and the quote. What do you think it means? Listen to an editorial about this idea. Were you right?**

" You now have the attention span of a goldfish. "

TIME magazine (May 2015)

🔊 2.10 Audio script

I have something to say, but you'll probably stop listening before I get to it. I know this because we humans have very short attention spans. It's true – well, according to *TIME* magazine. It seems we can't get anything done because we constantly **get interrupted** – by text messages, shopping alerts, that *ding* that says someone just updated their status – and find it impossible to **avoid distractions**.

According to the experts, our ability to **concentrate** is getting eaten away by technology and the tempting **distractions** it offers. It is increasingly difficult for us to **get focused** and **stay focused** for any length of time. In fact, your average person **loses focus** in just eight seconds – about the same as your average goldfish.

A goldfish? Really? I don't buy it. And neither does Dr. Gemma Briggs, a psychology professor who studies attention span and the things that **distract** us. In a television interview, she said, "How much attention we apply to a task will vary depending on what the task demand is," that is, on how difficult a task is to do.

This got me thinking about all the things demanding my attention these days – my job, the kids, the dog, not to mention my fantasy football team. Frankly, I'm a master of task-demand management. We all are. Our powers of **concentration** are stronger than ever because they have to be!

Take that, goldfish.

INSIDER ENGLISH

I don't buy it. = I don't believe it's true.

B 🔊 **2.10** [PAIR WORK] [THINK CRITICALLY] **Listen again and read. Why does the speaker think our powers of concentration have improved? Do you agree with him? Why or why not?**

2 VOCABULARY: Talking about attention and distraction

A 🔊 **2.11** [PAIR WORK] **Look at the bold words and phrases in the audio script. What do you think they mean? Use them to complete the chart below. Listen and check.**

Nouns	Verbs	Phrases
concentration	_____	
_____	_____	be / get distracted (by) _____ distractions
_____	focus (on)	get / _____ focused (on) lose focus
interruption	interrupt	be / _____ (by)

B ▶ **Now go to page 148. Do the vocabulary exercises for 8.1.**

C [PAIR WORK] **Discuss the questions.**

1 What thing(s) do you find most distracting? Why?

2 What tasks require a lot of concentration for you? What happens when you get interrupted?

3 How do you avoid distraction when you need to concentrate? Does it work?

> My phone is my main distraction. I get interrupted by messages and alerts all the time.

3 GRAMMAR: Phrases with *get*

A Read the sentences in the grammar box and notice the **bold** phrases. Then (circle) the correct options to complete the rules. Match each rule to a sentence.

> ### Phrases with *get*
>
> **A** We can't **get anything done** because we constantly get interrupted.
>
> **B** Our ability to concentrate **is getting eaten away** by technology.
>
> **C** It is increasingly difficult for us to **get focused** and stay focused.
>
> **D** This **got me thinking** about all the things demanding my attention.

The verb *get* is often used with other verbs. It can express different things depending on form and context.

1 To describe the completion of a task, use *get* + noun/pronoun + …   Sentence ___

  a past participle   **b** verb + *-ing*

2 To describe the changing state of something/somebody, use *get* + …   Sentence ___

  a past participle   **b** verb + *-ing*

3 To explain that something/somebody is prompting action, use
  get + noun/pronoun + …   Sentence ___

  a past participle   **b** verb + *-ing*

4 To describe a process in the passive, use *get* instead of *be*:
  get + noun/pronoun + … (+ *by* …)   Sentence ___

  a past participle   **b** verb + *-ing*

B 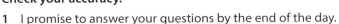 Now go to page 135. Look at the grammar chart and do the grammar exercise for 8.1.

C PAIR WORK Rephrase the sentences using a *get* phrase. Which ones could you restate using *have* instead of *get*? Check your accuracy.

1 I promise to answer your questions by the end of the day.

2 He has hired a professional designer to redecorate our new offices.

3 The interview made me wonder if I was the right person for the job.

4 I am becoming very frustrated with this computer program!

> ✓ **ACCURACY** CHECK
>
> To show that someone else will do a task, you can use *get* or *have*. If the subject is doing the action, however, use *get* only.
>
> *He can't ~~have~~ the printer to work.* ✗
> *He can't get the printer to work.* ✓
> *He's going to get / have it repaired.* ✓

4 SPEAKING

A PAIR WORK When you have a long to-do list, how do you prioritize the tasks? Do you stay focused and finish them all at once? What distractions or interruptions do you usually have to deal with? For ideas, watch Eric's video.

EXPERT SPEAKER

How could Eric avoid his biggest distraction?

B Share your experiences with the class. What gets done first on your to-do list? What, if you're honest, never gets done? Why?

> I like to **get the laundry done** on Sunday so I have clean clothes for the week. All the other jobs can **get pushed** to Monday or Tuesday.

GUT REACTION

1 LANGUAGE IN CONTEXT

A Look at the title of the article and read the quote. What do you think the article is about? Read the article and check your answer.

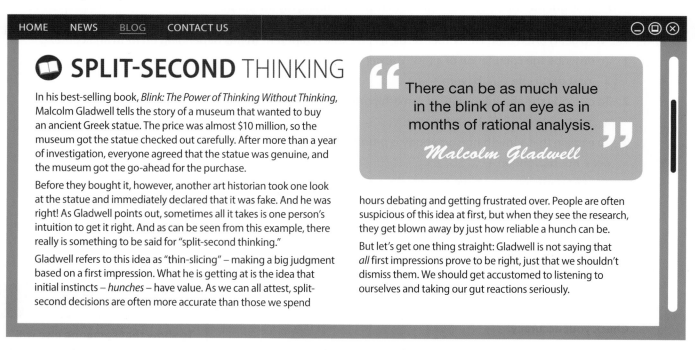

HOME   NEWS   BLOG   CONTACT US

📖 SPLIT-SECOND THINKING

In his best-selling book, *Blink: The Power of Thinking Without Thinking*, Malcolm Gladwell tells the story of a museum that wanted to buy an ancient Greek statue. The price was almost $10 million, so the museum got the statue checked out carefully. After more than a year of investigation, everyone agreed that the statue was genuine, and the museum got the go-ahead for the purchase.

Before they bought it, however, another art historian took one look at the statue and immediately declared that it was fake. And he was right! As Gladwell points out, sometimes all it takes is one person's intuition to get it right. And as can be seen from this example, there really is something to be said for "split-second thinking."

Gladwell refers to this idea as "thin-slicing" – making a big judgment based on a first impression. What he is getting at is the idea that initial instincts – *hunches* – have value. As we can all attest, split-second decisions are often more accurate than those we spend

> " There can be as much value in the blink of an eye as in months of rational analysis. "
>
> *Malcolm Gladwell*

hours debating and getting frustrated over. People are often suspicious of this idea at first, but when they see the research, they get blown away by just how reliable a hunch can be.

But let's get one thing straight: Gladwell is not saying that *all* first impressions prove to be right, just that we shouldn't dismiss them. We should get accustomed to listening to ourselves and taking our gut reactions seriously.

FIND IT

B **PAIR WORK** Read the article again. How many different expressions does the writer use to refer to "thinking without thinking"? List them. Use a dictionary or your phone to look up any terms you don't know.

2 VOCABULARY: Expressions with *get*

A 🔊 **2.12** **PAIR WORK** Listen to the expressions in the box. Then answer the questions.

get accustomed to	get at	get attached to	get blown away by
get complicated	get frustrated	get lost	get rid of
get something right	get something straight	get the go-ahead	

1 Which expressions are used in the article? Underline them.
2 Can you guess the meaning of the ones you don't know from the individual words?
3 In which expressions does *get* mean "become"? Circle them.

B ▶ Now go to page 148. Do the vocabulary exercises for 8.2.

C **PAIR WORK** **THINK CRITICALLY** What do you think about Gladwell's "thin-slicing" idea? Do you agree that it's a good thing? Give examples to support your ideas.

> I think it's good to **get accustomed to** trusting your instincts, even if you don't **get things right** all the time.

3 GRAMMAR: Phrases with *as*

A   Read the sentences in the grammar box and notice the **bold** phrases. Then complete the rules with the words in the box.

> **Phrases with *as***
>
> **As Gladwell points out**, sometimes all it takes is one person's intuition.
> **As can be seen from this example**, there really is something to be said for "split-second thinking."
> **As we can all attest**, split-second decisions are often more accurate.

evidence	illustrate	imagine	passive	statement

1   Phrases with *as* are used to support a _____ by referring to statistics, _____ , or shared experience or knowledge.

2   We often use phrases with *as* in the _____ to simplify and reduce introductory information, especially in formal writing or presentations.

3   When a phrase with *as* refers to the reader/listener, we often use these verbs: *attest, guess,* _____ , *infer, see.*

4   When a phrase with *as* refers to some type of support, we often use these verbs: *explain,* _____ , *indicate, point out, present, show, underline.*

B   ▶ **Now go to page 135. Do the grammar exercise for 8.2.**

C   PAIR WORK   **Look back at the audio script on page 76. Summarize the main points using phrases with *as*.**

> **As presented in the article in TIME magazine,** research suggests that a human's attention span is now shorter than that of a goldfish.

4 SPEAKING

A   PAIR WORK   **Think about different decisions: ordering food, choosing a vacation destination, shopping for clothes, etc. Do you usually go with your gut reaction? Why or why not?**

B   PAIR WORK   THINK CRITICALLY   **How do you make big decisions? Explain your process. Does it always result in the best choice?**

> Whenever I need new sneakers, I line up my options on the bench in the store. Then I **get rid of** the ones that are too expensive. Next, I ...

IT'S THE APP YOU NEED

LESSON OBJECTIVE
■ describe the best features and selling points of apps

FOCUS

1 LISTENING

A **PAIR WORK** Look at the app on the computer screen. It's designed to control other apps. How and why do you think it might do this?

B 🔊 **2.13** **LISTEN FOR MAIN POINTS** Listen to a conversation between Andrea, an app designer, and her friend Will. Were you right about the Focus app? How does it work?

C 🔊 **2.13** **LISTEN FOR DETAILS** Listen again and write specific information about the topics in the chart.

Topic	Details
A website blacklist	
The purpose of "locked mode"	
Target market	
The latest update	

D **PAIR WORK** Compare your charts. Did you both note the same details? Think about the app as Andrea describes it. Do you think it would work for you? Would you like to try it? Why or why not?

> **INSIDER ENGLISH**
>
> *go off the rails* = not go as planned
> *stay on track* = go according to plan

2 PRONUNCIATION: Listening for long word groups

A 🔊 **2.14** A *word group* has one main stress, and it is separated from the next word group by a slight pause. How many word groups are in the extracts?

1 Is that the think tank you were telling me about?

2 Then you create a "blacklist" of sites or tools that distract you the most.

3 No other app on the market offers a feature like this.

B 🔊 **2.15** **PAIR WORK** Listen and write down the number of words in each word group. Then listen again and write down all the words.

1 _____   4 _____

2 _____   5 _____

3 _____   6 _____

C Check (✓) the correct sentence.

☐ a Long word groups contain both stressed and unstressed words, and there is one tone movement.

☐ b All the words in long word groups are unstressed, and there are several tone movements.

3 SPEAKING SKILLS

A 🔊 2.13 PAIR WORK Listen to Andrea and Will's conversation again and complete the phrases for speaking persuasively.

Speak persuasively about a product

1 It _____ **users to** block distractions.

2 **That's the** _____ _____ **of** this new app.

3 **The** _____ _____ **is,** with this app, you can …

4 **What the app also** _____ **is** a way to …

5 **Our** _____ **is to** make this as customizable as possible.

6 **We're** _____ **to give users** all the flexibility they could possibly want.

7 _____ _____ _____ **on the market offers** a feature like this.

8 This **is a great** _____ **to** remove that temptation …

9 **You won't want to** _____ _____ **on** this great product.

10 **We're** _____ keeping you on track …

B PAIR WORK Think of an app that you really like and use regularly. Explain its best features and main selling points to your partner. Ask questions to learn more.

> I use an app called Skyscanner to find flights. Its main aim is to make searching for the right flight really easy.

> What's its best selling point?

> I'd say the route finder tool …

4 PRONUNCIATION: Saying primary and secondary word stress

A 🔊 2.16 Listen to the words. Circle the primary stress and underline the secondary stress.

1 opportunity   3 customizable   5 automatically
2 application   4 flexibility   6 notification

B 🔊 2.17 Choose the correct primary and secondary stress pattern. Listen and check.

1 a destination   b destination   4 a interruption   b interruption
2 a technological b technological   5 a concentration b concentration
3 a responsibility b responsibility   6 a intuition   b intuition

C PAIR WORK Complete the sentences with one of the words from exercise 4A or 4B. Read the sentences out loud and discuss them.

1 People in the past had better _____ because there were fewer distractions.

2 Parents have a _____ to make sure their children don't become too dependent on digital devices.

3 The _____ of electronic books makes them more appealing than print books to many customers.

4 Technology means that anyone with internet access has the _____ to get a great education.

5 SPEAKING

A GROUP WORK THINK CRITICALLY How much time, energy, or money do you think apps really save? If you could only download three apps, what would they be? What purpose(s) would they serve?

> My commuter app doesn't save me time, but it prevents me from getting frustrated because of a late train.

8.4 THE PERFECT PITCH

1 READING

A **PAIR WORK** Make a list of all the different ways people and companies sell things today. Go online to find even more. Which have you experienced?

B Read the title and introduction to the article. What is an "elevator pitch"? Why is it called that? Why is it so important? How is a pitch different from a presentation? Read the rest of the article to check your answers.

SIX TIPS FOR THE PERFECT PITCH

When you meet a potential investor, it is crucial to be able to get your message across in no more time than it would take to ride up an elevator together. To get your "elevator pitch" just right, take some tips from entrepreneurs who have mastered the art of the perfect pitch.

TIP 1 Keep it short and sweet.

Keep in mind that investors typically watch hundreds of presentations. To stand out from the competition, think of an intriguing mission statement that features your product and states why it is unique. A good example of a catchy mission statement is Google's "to organize the world's information and make it universally accessible." You can't argue with that!

TIP 2 Solve a problem.

Know your potential investor and focus your pitch on their interests. Highlight why *your* company provides a unique solution to a problem they might have. Here, it's important to focus on positive aspects, such as growth and risk protection. This way, you'll anticipate your investor's concerns and give them the answer before they have to ask you.

TIP 3 Practice, practice, practice.

When you speak in public, you need to be confident and sure of your facts. Have everything crystal clear in your mind and anticipate difficult questions or surprising reactions. The best way to do this? Practice as much as you can. The good thing about practicing an elevator pitch is that it's short – you can do it again and again. If you're succinct and get to the point fast, you'll do fine!

TIP 4 Use an analogy.

Pitches often include abstract concepts that can be difficult for people to grasp. An image or an analogy can help explain your idea. A good example comes from Trello, a web-based app that helps organize projects into different boards, like "sticky notes on a wall." This conjures up a familiar image and makes the idea clearer and more accessible.

TIP 5 Read the crowd.

Although you only have a minute or so, it's important to read your audience and react accordingly. There's no point in following your script, however brilliant it might be, if it isn't going well. If things are going off the rails, reshape your pitch based on the signals your audience is giving you. Be spontaneous and respond to the here and now.

TIP 6 Make it personal.

To be truly convincing, you need to talk from the heart. If you don't bring personality and passion into your pitch, your potential investor will lose interest. People don't just invest in an idea or a product, they invest in the people behind it. If you are truly excited about your big new idea, your enthusiasm will get them excited, too.

Follow these tips, and potential investors will know you mean business – in more ways than one!

C **EVALUATE INFORMATION** Read the article again. Indicate which tips address the different aspects of an elevator pitch below.

Aspects of an elevator pitch	Tip 1	Tip 2	Tip 3	Tip 4	Tip 5	Tip 6
1 your knowledge of the product or idea	✓	✓	✓			
2 listener interaction						
3 your delivery						
4 content						

D **PAIR WORK** **THINK CRITICALLY** Which tips do you think apply to any type of public speaking? Which tip(s) do you find most useful for yourself? Why?

> I think practice is important to overcome nerves. If you speak smoothly, it will help your confidence. That's important whenever you speak in public.

2 WRITING

A **PAIR WORK** Look at two slides from a presentation about the article "Six Tips for the Perfect Pitch." Compare the language used in the original article with the language used in the presentation slides. What are the main differences?

TIP **1**

LENGTH
- Keep it short & sweet
- Mission statement crucial
- Stand out from the rest

Mission statement example
"to organize the world's information and make it universally accessible" – Google

TIP **4**

ANALOGY
- Don't use abstract ideas
- Make your message more direct and accessible with an image

Analogy example:
"sticky notes on wall" – Trello

B **PAIR WORK** Think about the different elements of a presentation slide and answer the questions.

1 Why use bullet points?
2 What is the relationship between the text on the slide and what the presenter says?
3 What are some ways to enliven presentation slides without distracting the viewer from what the speaker is saying?

C **ADAPT CONTENT** Look at your chart in exercise 1C again, and then complete this slide about the first aspect of a good elevator pitch. Be as succinct as possible. Compare slides with a partner. Which of you was more succinct?

KNOW YOUR PRODUCT

- Practice!
- Keep it [1] _____
- Create a [2] _____
- Anticipate [3] _____
- Be [4] _____ of your facts

"To organize the world's information and make it universally accessible" – Google

 **WRITE IT**

FIND IT

D **PLAN** You're going to create a presentation about the most important aspects of a good elevator pitch. With a partner, compare charts from exercise 1C and resolve any disagreements about how the information in the article relates to the categories in the chart.

E Follow the steps to create your presentation. Your slides should contain no more than 120 words total.

■ Make one introduction slide.
■ Make four content slides, one for each aspect presented in the chart. (You can use the slide in exercise 2C as your first content slide.) Go online and do some research of your own, if you can.
■ Make one ending slide.
■ Add images, quotes, and statistics to make your slides more interesting.
■ Review the slides from exercise 2A and compare your slides to them. Are your points presented succinctly? Are your slides graphically interesting?

F **GROUP WORK** Join another pair of students and share your slide presentations. How are your slides similar? How are they different? Whose presentation do you think would be more interesting?

TIME TO SPEAK
Make a pitch

- pitch a company, an idea, or a product to investors

A **PREPARE** Look at the picture. With a partner, discuss what had to happen before these entrepreneurs could open their new cafe. Write down all the stages. How much time do you think each stage took? Who did they need to talk to, and why? How much money did it take to get to their big grand opening?

B Join another pair of students and form a small group. Compare the stages you thought of in exercise A. Did you both come up with a similar process? Then look at the products below that would likely need investment to get started. Think of more and add them to the list.

customizable sneakers

a service to help new students set up their dorm rooms

vegan coffee shop near a university

C **PLAN** Choose one of the products from exercise B to pitch to investors. Start planning your pitch by identifying key information:

- the problem(s) that your product/service will solve
- an analogy that will make the idea accessible
- the main selling points of your product/service
- questions people might ask
- a mission statement

Write your pitch in bullet-point format on index cards, and create presentation slides if you can. Remember, however, that these are only cues to help guide your presentation. You will not read them aloud. Decide who will present which parts of your pitch. Practice the transitions from one speaker to the next.

D **PRACTICE** Work with another group and present your pitches to each other. Offer and listen to feedback. Then work in your original group again to refine your pitch.

E **PRESENT** Pitch your idea to the "investors" (the class). Use visuals if you can to support your presentation. Ask questions when you're an investor.

F **AGREE** Discuss which pitches were the most interesting. Which products or services were the most original? Which idea would you like to invest in, and why?

>> To check your progress, go to page 155.

USEFUL PHRASES

PLAN

What's a unique selling point for our product?

… is something no other product on the market can offer right now.

I think … should present the details because I'll get confused if people ask questions.

AGREE

I love the idea of … – it's simple but exciting.

I don't think there's much of a market for …

84

UNIT OBJECTIVES

- discuss the effects of a sedentary lifestyle
- suggest ways to establish good sleep habits
- ask and deflect probing questions
- write about a clean-water initiative and how it works
- present and explain choices that you have made for other people

START SPEAKING

A **Look at the picture. What is this man doing? Why do you think he's doing it in this location and not in the mountains? Is this location just as good? Why or why not?**

B **What does the picture suggest to you about staying fit and healthy in cities? What are some health advantages and disadvantages of life in an urban environment?**

C **What advice would you give for enjoying city life and staying healthy? For ideas, watch Audrey's video.**

EXPERT SPEAKER

How important is Audrey's point for you personally?

9.1 THE SITTING DISEASE

1 LANGUAGE IN CONTEXT

A **Look at the pictures and the title of the article. How do they relate to each other? What do you expect to learn about in this article? Read and check your answers.**

Sitting – a growing health risk for all ages

New evidence suggests that 19-year-olds spend as much time sitting as 60-year-olds, and that the "sitting disease" is something that affects all of us, from preschool to retirement.

A **sedentary lifestyle** has well-known medical **side effects**. It increases **blood pressure** and **cholesterol levels** and the risk of **cardiovascular disease**. It has a negative effect on **posture**, putting pressure on **internal organs**, which has a knock-on effect on **digestion**. It causes **chronic pain** in **joints**, negatively affects **circulation**, and even compromises the **immune system**. This doesn't make for a big news story, but the fact that the sitting disease now affects *all ages* does.

It's worrying to think that even young children are not getting enough exercise, but a solution to the problem may lie in creative alternatives to traditional desks and chairs.

Standing desks alleviate the stress on the back, neck, and internal organs. Stand-up meetings give similar results.

By trading standard chairs for exercise balls and installing pedal desks, schools make it easy for students to stay active and be focused at the same time. Adopting treadmill desks allows companies to do the same for their employees.

The balls force users to sit up straight, which keeps them alert, and the action of pedaling or walking not only gets them moving, it also means they stay physically and mentally engaged with their work.

We may not be able to cut the number of hours we spend at work or school, but sitting all day is something we don't have to stand for anymore!

B **PAIR WORK** **Are you surprised by any of the information in the text? Which type of alternative furniture would you like to try out? Why?**

INSIDER ENGLISH

knock-on effect = indirect consequence of an action

2 VOCABULARY: Discussing health issues

FIND IT

A 🔊 **2.18** **PAIR WORK** **Look at the bold words in the article. What do they mean? Use a dictionary or your phone to help you. Write them in the correct categories in the chart below. Then listen and check.**

Features of the body	Factors associated with the "sitting disease"
blood pressure	sedentary lifestyle

B ▶ **Now go to page 149. Do the vocabulary exercises for 9.1.**

C **PAIR WORK** **THINK CRITICALLY** **How can people add physical activity into their daily routines? What could workplaces, schools, and the government do to help? Do you think these measures would be enough to balance out a sedentary lifestyle?**

3 GRAMMAR: Referencing

A Look at the extracts from the article in the grammar box. Then complete the rules below.

> **Referencing**
>
> **This** (*the knowledge of side effects of a sedentary lifestyle*) doesn't make for a big news story, but the fact that the sitting disease now affects all ages **does** (*make this a big news story*).
>
> **It**'s worrying to think that even young children are not getting enough exercise.
>
> Stand-up meetings give **similar results** (*to those of standing desks*).
>
> By installing pedal desks, schools make it easy for students to stay active. Adopting treadmill desks allows companies to **do the same** for their employees. (*make it easy to stay active*)
>
> The action of pedaling or walking not only gets **them** (*users*) moving, **it** also means **they** (*users*) stay physically and mentally engaged with **their** (*the users'*) work.

Referencing techniques make it possible to avoid repetition in your writing.

To avoid repeating a noun or concept mentioned earlier in the same text …

- use possessive adjectives (such as *its* or ¹_____).
- use pronouns (such as *it*, ²_____ , *them*, or *this*).
- use phrases like *the same* or ³_____ + noun.

To avoid repeating a verb, use an auxiliary verb such as *be*, *have*, or ⁴_____ in the correct form.

B ▶ Now go to page 136. Look at the grammar chart and do the grammar exercise for 9.1.

C PAIR WORK Take turns and talk about one of the topics below for 30 seconds without repeating any of the bold words. Your partner will time you.

- the **bike-sharing** program in [**name of our city**]
- **walking** up the **stairs** instead of taking the **elevator**
- using a **standing desk** at work
- **sitting on an exercise ball** when you **watch TV**

> I think **this** is a great idea. **It** makes a lot of sense. The vehicles people ride are easy to use, and you can find **them** all over Quito. A lot of people use **this** program. I **do**, too.

> Oh, no! You said "Quito." Start over!

4 SPEAKING

A GROUP WORK Choose one of the groups below and think of three ways they could discourage a sedentary lifestyle.

- teachers of young children
- parents of teenagers
- companies that employ a lot of office staff

B Share your ideas with the class. Who has the most creative suggestions?

> Companies could provide yoga classes that help you have good **posture** …

A GOOD NIGHT'S SLEEP

LESSON OBJECTIVE
■ suggest ways to establish good sleep habits

1 LANGUAGE IN CONTEXT

A 🔊 **2.19** Look at the infographic. What are the main physical benefits of getting a good night's sleep? In what ways do you think modern life interferes with sleep? Listen to part of a podcast. Are any of your ideas mentioned?

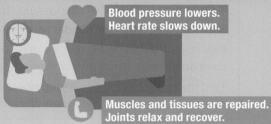

THE BENEFITS OF A GOOD NIGHT'S SLEEP

Memories are processed and stored. Growth hormones are released.

Blood pressure lowers. Heart rate slows down.

Muscles and tissues are repaired. Joints relax and recover.

🔊 **2.19 Audio script**

GLOSSARY
flip side (*n*) the opposite result of a good situation

Host	Before the break, Dr. Raymond Shaw talked about the benefits of good sleep, but now we're going to be looking at the flip side – the dangers of sleep deprivation. We all know lack of sleep is dangerous, so why do we *still* not get enough of it?
Shaw	Well, first off, we seem to be packing way too much into our days. We get up too early and go to bed too late. We know we need to be racking up at least seven hours of sleep a night, but it's hard to fit those seven hours into our busy schedules.
Host	So, what might be stopping us? And what can we do about it?
Shaw	Well, physical stimulants don't help, so we should try to cut out caffeine and sugar, or at least cut back on them. Also, the pressure of work or school means tension builds up during the day, making it harder to wind down at night. But the main thing keeping us up is FOMO.
Host	FOMO? You mean, *Fear Of Missing Out*?
Shaw	Uh-huh. That's what drives us to our screens late at night – social media updates, breaking news stories, the latest Tweets. We kid ourselves that we're just taking a quick peek before we drift off to sleep, but time just slips away. Those minutes add up to hours, and soon you're watching cat videos when you should be sleeping!

B **PAIR WORK** **THINK CRITICALLY** Do you agree that FOMO is a big factor in bad sleeping habits? Why or why not? Is it a problem for you? For ideas, watch Audrey's video.

EXPERT SPEAKER

Are you more like Audrey or the people she describes?

2 VOCABULARY: Discussing (lack of) sleep

A 🔊 **2.20** **PAIR WORK** Listen to the phrasal verbs in the box and then find them in the audio script above. Can you figure out their meaning from context? How would you rephrase them using different words?

add up	build up	cut back on	cut out
drift off	drive somebody to	fit something into	keep somebody up
pack something into	rack up	slip away	wind down

B ▶ Now go to page 149. Do the vocabulary exercises for 9.2.

C **PAIR WORK** Discuss the questions. Use phrasal verbs from the box above in your answers.

■ How many hours of sleep do you normally get per night? Is it different on weekends?

■ Do you ever find it difficult to get to sleep at night? What kinds of things keep you up?

■ Would you agree that sleep deprivation is an inevitable consequence of modern life? Why or why not?

3 GRAMMAR: Continuous infinitives

A **Look at the sentences in the grammar box. Complete the rules.**

> **Continuous infinitives**
>
> We're going **to be looking** at the flip side.
>
> We seem **to be packing** way too much into our days.
>
> We know we need **to be racking up** at least seven hours of sleep a night.
>
> You're watching cat videos when you **should be sleeping**!

1 A continuous infinitive is formed with *to* + _____ + verb + *-ing*. It emphasizes that an action is in progress over a period of time.

2 It is used with the verbs *appear* and _____ to comment on ongoing actions and situations.

3 It is used with the verbs *want*, *would like*, and _____ to comment on intentions and plans.

4 It is used with the modals _____ , *could*, and *might* to criticize or speculate about an ongoing action or situation.

B ▶ **Now go to page 137. Look at the grammar chart and do the grammar exercise for 9.2**

C PAIR WORK **Complete the sentences with the correct verb in the continuous infinitive, and check your accuracy. Which statements do you agree with? Why?**

> ✓ **ACCURACY** CHECK
>
> The linking verbs *need* and *seem* are always followed by an infinitive form of a verb.
>
> *Traffic seems ~~moving~~ fairly smoothly.* ✗
> *Traffic seems to be moving fairly smoothly.* ✓

| ask | get worse | sacrifice | sleep |

1 People seem _____ sleep in order to binge-watch their favorite shows as soon as a new season is released.

2 Doctors need _____ their patients about sleep and other lifestyle issues. This information will alert them to possible health problems.

3 I'd love _____ right now. In general, I'd rather sleep fewer hours at night and take naps during the day.

4 Since I started college, the situation with sleep deprivation seems _____ .

4 SPEAKING

A GROUP WORK **Look at the descriptions of different categories of people. Add another one to the list. What do you think each group needs to be doing to make sure they get enough sleep?**

- high school students who rack up too many hours online
- people who have to fit a lot into a day, like parents with young children and full-time jobs
- doctors and first responders who are on call at all hours and find it difficult to wind down and relax
- _____

B **Tell the class what advice you came up with for each group.**

> We think parents need **to be monitoring** how much time their kids spend online. If it gets too extreme, they should make them **cut back on** screen time.

9.3 CLEARING THE AIR

1 LISTENING

A 🔊 **2.21** **Look at the pictures of two major industries in California. What are they? What effect do you think they have on air quality? Listen to an interview with an administrator from Waylons, California, and check your answers.**

B 🔊 **2.21** **LISTEN FOR PURPOSE** Listen again. Is the administrator interested in finding solutions to the air quality issues? How do you know? Is the interviewer satisfied with the administrator's answers? Why do you think that?

C 🔊 **2.22** **PAIR WORK** Look at some of the questions the interviewer asks. Listen and note what the **bold** words refer to. Compare your answers with a partner. Listen again if needed.

1   Isn't it fair to say that **the situation** is critical here at the moment?

2   Wouldn't you agree that this is **an issue** that deserves attention?

3   Are you suggesting that there's nothing that can be done to regulate **those industries**?

4   Is **that** a policy your department supports?

5   What's your reaction to **that**?

6   Is **that story** not true?

7   Is **that** the administration's position?

D **PAIR WORK** **THINK CRITICALLY** How does your hometown compare with Waylons in terms of industrialization, air quality, and the local government response to environmental and health issues?

2 PRONUNCIATION: Listening for stressed and unstressed grammar words

A 🔊 **2.23** **Listen. In which sentence is the underlined word stressed?**

1   a   … the current administration in Washington is planning to relax those regulations, and that <u>could</u>, in fact, make matters worse …

    b   I'm sorry, but <u>could</u> you give me some concrete examples?

2   a   What <u>do</u> you mean?

    b   … but I <u>do</u> know that there are a lot of interesting initiatives being explored …

B 🔊 **2.24** **Complete the sentences. Which word should be stressed? Listen and check.**

1   I'm afraid I _____ comment on federal legislation. But I _____ say we're doing everything we can to make sure that industries abide by the state and local regulations currently in place.

2   _____'s not what activist groups are saying. They claim _____ your department is pro-industry and anti-community.

C Circle the correct words to complete the sentence.

Grammar words are usually ¹*stressed / unstressed*, but they are ²*stressed / unstressed* to emphasize a point.

3 SPEAKING SKILLS

A 🔊 **2.21** [PAIR WORK] **Read and complete the sentences from the interview in the chart. Listen again and write down more examples of each type. Compare the examples you found with a partner and read them aloud to each other. Be sure to stress the main word in complex noun phrases.**

Asking probing questions	Buying time to think / deflecting questions
Surely you can't be suggesting that … ?	I'm glad you brought that up …
Isn't it [1]_____ to say that … ?	Well, that's an interesting point …
Wouldn't you [2]_____ that … ?	[6]_____ ?
How do you explain the fact that … ?	[7]_____
[3]_____ ?	[8]_____
[4]_____ ?	[9]_____
[5]_____ ?	[10]_____

B [PAIR WORK] **Imagine the situations below. Would you be more likely to ask probing questions or deflect questions in each one? Why? Act out one of the situations for another pair of students.**

- a conversation with a friend
- a heated argument with your roommates
- a question-and-answer session after a presentation
- a meeting with your parents about your grades

4 PRONUNCIATION: Saying consonant clusters

A 🔊 **2.25** **Listen to some common consonant clusters and example words. Repeat them.**

/str/ straightforward   /kw/ quality   /kr/ concrete   /sp/ spokesperson

/pr/ preventable   /nts/ pollutants   /tr/ control   /bl/ blocking

B 🔊 **2.26** **Listen and write in the missing words you hear. Practice the conversation with a partner. Does your partner pronounce the consonant clusters clearly?**

A Well, there is too much [1]_____ . That's [2]_____ obvious.

B But we can't just ask people to stop driving! That's too extreme.

A We could [3]_____ heavy [4]_____ from the city. That would be a start.

B Interesting idea, but I'm not sure the solution is that [5]_____ .

C [GROUP WORK] **Add six more lines to the conversation, using consonant clusters from exercise 4A in every line. Join another pair and read your conversations. What consonant clusters did they use? Does everyone pronounce the consonant clusters clearly?**

5 SPEAKING

A [PAIR WORK] **Choose one of the issues in the box or another that you know something about. Discuss the main problems in relation to your town and take notes.**

noise pollution   pollution from industry   residential recycling   traffic

B [PAIR WORK] **Act out a discussion between a reporter and a local politician about the issue you chose.**

I'd like to start by asking why your administration is cutting funding for recycling?

Well, I'm not sure that's totally accurate. I mean, the situation isn't quite as simple as that.

But isn't it true that you have slashed the recycling budget by more than 50 percent?

A THIRSTY WORLD

1 READING

A   **PAIR WORK**   **Look at the pictures. What do they have in common? What do they tell us about issues with water today?**

B   **Read the titles of three short articles. What aspect of the water crisis do you think each one will cover?**

a   Big business giving back

b   Star power in the fight for clean water

c   The water crisis: Facts and figures

C   **IDENTIFY PURPOSE**   **Read the stories and write in the correct titles from exercise 1B. From whose point of view is each story being told? Which stories do you think give a balanced account of the situation? Why?**

| Home | Health | Business | Politics | World | More ▾ |

Water is essential to life, we all know that. But access to water is something most of us take for granted. Around the world, one in nine people do not have access to safe, clean water supplies. In countries where water is scarce, 80 percent of illnesses are linked to poor water quality and lack of proper sanitation. Providing access to clean water could save as many as two million lives every year.

Clean water would also have dramatic effects on the lives of millions of people, especially women and children. In the most badly affected areas, they spend up to six hours a day simply providing water for their families. Their lives are sacrificed to the daily chore of collecting water. Children have no time to go to school, and women can't pursue work outside the home, creating a cycle of poverty in the community.

Help us fight this global crisis. Click here to donate.

Source: businessconnectworld.com

More and more celebrities are using their fame to promote water charities and raise money to solve water issues around the world. But does celebrity appeal really work? We look at two examples.

1   Matt Damon, known for such movie roles as Jason Bourne, was one of the first celebrities to use his fame to bring attention to clean water issues. In 2009 he co-founded a water charity called Water.org that provides microloans to families in developing countries to connect to water and sanitation systems or build their own. The organization has helped more than seven million people around the world.

2   NFL star Chris Long was so struck by the problems he saw when he visited Tanzania to climb Kilimanjaro that he started a charity called Waterboys. Along with fellow football players recruited by Long, the foundation raises money to provide safe, clean water throughout East Africa. In its first two years, the charity raised enough money to build 23 wells and provide water for more than 100,000 people.

Sources: globalcitizen.org; waterboys.org

The Coca-Cola Company is committed to working with communities in need all over the world. It has set up a number of collaborative projects with local and global charities to join the fight in making the world a better place.

In India and Africa, Coca-Cola is currently involved in two major projects to provide clean drinking water for poor communities. The Support My School program in India is building modern bathrooms with access to clean water in hundreds of schools, improving sanitary conditions and school attendance for nearly 100,000 students.

In Africa, the corporation is investing heavily in RAIN (the Replenish Africa Initiative), with the aim of building new wells and providing access to clean water for two million people over the coming years.

Through these and other projects, Coca-Cola is helping fight poverty on the front lines: reducing the incidence of waterborne diseases, keeping children – especially girls – in school, and empowering parents to pursue a better life for their families.

Sources: worldvision.org/corporate/; The Coca-Cola Foundation

D   **PAIR WORK**   **THINK CRITICALLY**   **Why do celebrities and big corporations get involved with charitable projects? Are they motivated by the same things?**

2 WRITING

A **Reread the story in exercise 1C about Water.org's initiative. How is it different from the other initiatives? Then read the paragraph below. Does it explain the nature of the organization accurately and completely?**

Water.org does not provide people with clean water, **per se**. It does not drill wells, build sanitation facilities, or provide water pipes. It does something that is, **at its heart**, much more important. It empowers people to solve problems for themselves and take the matter of access to clean water into their own hands. The problem is, **inherently**, a financial one. **More often than not**, people who spend hours every day in search of water do not have time to work and can't make or save the money they need to pay for clean water. It's a vicious cycle, but money, **in and of itself**, won't break it. By offering families microloans to establish a reliable connection to clean water sources, Water.org is, **fundamentally**, investing in communities, giving them the power to invest in themselves.

FIND IT

B **Look at the bold words in the paragraph above. Which terms in the box have a similar meaning and could replace them? More than one option might be possible. Use a dictionary or your phone to help you.**

| as a matter of course | as such | by definition | by its very nature | essentially | intrinsically |

C **EXPLAIN DISTINCTIONS** Complete the sentences with adverbials from exercises 2A and 2B. More than one option may be possible.

1 Microloans are, _____ , a tool for empowerment.

2 Microloans are not enough, _____ . People also need to find a way to make money to be able to pay back the loans.

3 Freeing people from the chore of finding water is, _____ , giving them a chance to live a better life.

4 Access to clean, safe water is, _____ , the basis of a happy and healthy life.

WRITE IT

FIND IT

D **PLAN You're going to write an explanatory paragraph about another solution to the problem of clean water from the LifeStraw organization. With a partner, look at the diagram and discuss how the device works.**

Ultrafiltration membrane cartridge inside

Safe water tap

Prefilter

Dirty water storage tank

Safe water storage tank

In what ways is this initiative different from the other ones presented in this lesson? You can use your phone to do more research if you want.

E **Write your paragraph in 120–150 words. Use adverbial expressions from exercises 2A and 2B.**

F **PAIR WORK Read each other's paragraphs. Offer and listen to feedback and revise your work.**

TIME TO SPEAK
Desert island dilemma

A | **RESEARCH** What are the best things about modern life? With a partner, make a list of your ideas. Look at the pictures to help you. Then write 6–10 survey questions to find out what your classmates think.

B | Interview another pair of students. Ask your questions and take careful notes.

C | **DISCUSS** Read the announcement.

> Two students have been chosen to live on an isolated island for two years as part of an experiment. Only basic food supplies and shelters are provided. Study participants may bring one thing with them.

The students you just interviewed are the study participants, but you will choose the one thing they can take to the island. Consider the following questions and consult your notes to reach a decision.

■ What will each person miss most?
■ Could they find or make substitutes on the island?
■ Should each person take something that they both can use?

D | **PRACTICE** Present your choices and the reasons for them to another pair of students – not the study participants. Listen to their feedback. Revise your proposal.

E | **PRESENT** Focusing on your study participants but in front of the whole class, share your decision and explain your choices. Are your study participants happy with your choices for them? Are you happy with their choices for you?

>> *To check your progress, go to page 155.* >>

USEFUL PHRASES

DISCUSS

What will … miss most about … ?

… loves … , but he could use … as a substitute.

If we let her take … , they could both use it.

PRACTICE

… appears to be studying … in her free time, so …

… will be taking … because he'll miss … more than anything else.

People need to be doing something, or they go crazy. Maybe think about …

REVIEW 3 (UNITS 7–9)

1 VOCABULARY

A Complete the conversation with the correct words.

concentrating | keep alive | ethnic
interrupt | rituals | mark | focused
distracted | genealogy | ancestors
inherited | festivities

Marcia Ted, do you have any interest in ¹_____ _____?

Ted Funny you should ask that. The other day, my mother was telling me about some family research she's been doing – our ²_____ and our ³_____ background, etc. It was really interesting, but I couldn't stay ⁴_____. My boss kept texting me, and I'd get ⁵_____ and miss what she was saying.

Marcia I know the feeling! The other day I was with my family – it was my parents' anniversary, and we ⁶_____ the occasion every year with a little party. I really like how we ⁷_____ that tradition _____, especially now that there are grandkids. Anyway, I noticed that everybody was ⁸_____ on their phones rather than the conversation.

Ted Were your parents upset by that?

Marcia Not really. But it was a special day, and I didn't want beeps and buzzes to ⁹_____ the ¹⁰_____, so I told everyone to put their phones away. And they did. It was nice.

Ted That's great. Those family ¹¹_____ are so important. The kids will realize that one day. Oh, and guess what I learned! My great-great-grandmother had bright red hair, so that must be who I ¹²_____ mine from.

B [PAIR WORK] Think about an occasion or practice that your family observes together. Does it have significance for other people, too? When you're all together, does everyone put their phones away? Why or why not? Does anyone get upset about it?

2 GRAMMAR

A Rewrite the sentences using the words in parentheses ( ).

1 I never would have thought that my parents' native language could die out. (*Never* …)

2 After the article was published in the newspaper, then I realized my mistake. (*Only* …)

3 The memories of ancient festivals linger in the town square. (*In* …)

4 The remains of last night's celebration lie on the city streets. (*On the* …)

5 That documentary made me think I should donate money to water charities. (*… got me* …)

6 I haven't been able to do any work this morning. (*… get* …)

B [PAIR WORK] **Change your sentences from exercise 2A so that they say something true about you and your experience.**

Never would I have guessed that my grandmother likes rock music, but she does! I just learned that she went to concerts all the time in the '60s and '70s!

3 VOCABULARY

A (Circle) the correct terms to complete the advice column.

ASK DR. OLIVIA WATTS

| Home | New posts | Forum |

Q ⊙ Profile

 Brian, Chicago, 2:45 p.m.
I'm 42 and starting to notice changes in my
¹*circulation / posture*. Sometimes, I can't stand up
straight. Any good advice for me?

 Dr. Watts
Do you have a ²*chronic pain / sedentary lifestyle*?
I'll bet you do. You need to get ³*rid of / attached to*
your traditional desk and invest in something
better. Physical therapy can help, although many
people get ⁴*frustrated / complicated* when they
don't see immediate results. Be patient. If you
haven't had a general physical exam in a while,
get one. As we get older, it's important to monitor
things like ⁵*immune system / cholesterol levels* and
weight and adjust our diet accordingly. Take care
of yourself!

 Celia, Santiago, 6:02 a.m.
I have ⁶*high blood pressure / side effects*. It's an inherited
condition, but isn't there something I can be doing to
reduce it? I'm really scared.

 Dr. Watts
Celia, let's get something ⁷*straight / right* – you can't cure
this condition, but you absolutely can improve it with
behavior changes. First, try to ⁸*build up / cut back on*
fatty foods as much as possible. You also need to reduce
stress. Learning how to ⁹*wind down / slip away* in the
evening so that you fall asleep faster is fundamental.
We're all busy, but it's so important to ¹⁰*fit / break* some
exercise *into* your daily routine, even just walking.
Get a dog! That will force you to walk.

Take control! Talk to your doctor, make a plan, and stick
to it.

B PAIR WORK **Have you or has anyone you know suffered from these complaints? Which one? Is the doctor's
advice good? Why or why not? What advice would you give Brian and Celia?**

4 GRAMMAR

A **Complete the sentences from an essay about medical advice websites with the phrases in the box.**

| appear to be | can all attest | points out | should be getting |
| to be looking at | to be suggesting | you can see | |

1 As _____ from the questions in the "Ask Dr. Olivia Watts" example, people know their health
   issues, but they don't know how to get help with *these issues*.

2 As the doctor _____ , diet is very important. In fact, some doctors say *diet* is the most significant
   factor in maintaining good health.

3 As we _____ , being constantly mindful of health issues isn't easy or fun, but *thinking about
   health* is necessary if we want to have a good life.

4 Another important factor is sleep. Based on clinical studies, researchers assert that we _____
   at least seven hours per night, and based on experience, doctors report *identical findings to those of the researchers*.

5 The research seems _____ that kids need even more. Teenagers function better if they get nine
   hours of sleep a night, and younger children *function better with nine hours of sleep*, too.

6 Teenagers may believe they can catch up on sleep on the weekend, but many experts *feel this is not true*. Though teens might
   _____ well rested, oversleeping actually makes them more tired the next day.

7 We are going _____ two studies from Canada that back up this assertion and two others from
   Brazil that produced *not identical but closely correlated* results.

B PAIR WORK **Look at the sentences in exercise 4A and replace the *italicized* words with an appropriate referent
to avoid repetition.**

UNIT OBJECTIVES

- talk about future food options and how likely they are
- discuss new ways to use natural energy sources
- discuss the advantages of rethinking daily habits
- write a summary of a discussion about the new economy
- present and evaluate an idea for reinventing pet ownership

START SPEAKING

A Look at the picture. What has been reinvented? In what way? How might this change the whole idea and experience of driving? Do you think the design will become a reality? Why or why not?

B What things do you think will be dramatically reimagined in the next 10 to 20 years? What do you expect to stay the same forever? Why?

C Think of something that you've reinvented. What changes did you make to it, and why? How extreme was your reinvention? What do people think of it? For ideas, watch Ryoko's video.

EXPERT SPEAKER

What do you think of Ryoko's reinvention? How extreme is it?

10.1 BUGS NOT BEEF

LESSON OBJECTIVE
- talk about future food options and how likely they are

1 LANGUAGE IN CONTEXT

A 🔊 **2.27** **Look at the picture. What type of insect is this? Where can you find them? Have you ever eaten one? If not, would you consider it? Listen to the news story. Were your answers correct?**

🔊 **2.27 Audio script**

We all love food, but our **consumption** of it will soon overwhelm both **supply** and production. Take meat, for example. Animal agriculture will increase at least 70 percent by 2050. Already, one-third of the world's **grains** and **cereals** are used to feed **livestock**, and **cattle** farming alone occupies 24 percent of land globally. It takes 15,000 liters of water to produce one kilogram of beef, so greater production means more water **shortages** worldwide.

Imagine if we could reduce our **appetite** for this inefficient protein source. Though some people would rather we gave up meat altogether, most agree that it's time we started exploring alternatives.

This idea is what led Brown University students Gabi Lewis and Greg Sewitz to buy 2,000 live crickets in 2013. Insects are common **foodstuffs** in many parts of the world, but not in the U.S. and Canada. So they wondered, *What if we created a cool new food product to introduce insect protein to people here?* With only a basic recipe for cricket flour, Lewis and Sewitz created a company – Exo. Today, Exo offers many healthy food products, including their popular protein bars made with cricket flour.

Crickets are **wholesome** and **nutritious**, with essential proteins, **fiber**, and twice as much iron as spinach. They're super green, too – making food from crickets uses just one liter of water per kilogram. Crickets might just be the new **superfood**.

B **PAIR WORK** **THINK CRITICALLY** **What are the environmental advantages of using insects such as crickets as food? What protein alternatives to beef and other livestock meats can you think of? What environmental advantages might they have?**

2 VOCABULARY: Discussing global food issues

A 🔊 **2.28** **PAIR WORK** **Look at the bold words in the article. Write them in the correct category below. Then listen and check.**

1 related to food quantity: _____ , _____
2 non-meat foods: _____ and _____ , which both contain _____
3 describing the healthfulness of food: _____ , _____
4 collective words for animals we eat: _____ , _____
5 other ways to categorize things we eat: _____ , _____
6 related to eating: _____ , _____

B ▶ **Now go to page 150. Do the vocabulary exercises for 10.1.**

FIND IT

C **GROUP WORK** **How is a superfood different from regular foodstuffs? Use your phone to help you. What other superfoods are there? For ideas, watch Ryoko's video.**

EXPERT SPEAKER

What do you think of Ryoko's alternative to eating superfoods?

3 GRAMMAR: Simple past for unreal situations

A Look at the sentences in the grammar box. In each sentence, what is the use of the <u>underlined</u> simple past verb? Match the sentences to the use(s) below.

> **Simple past for unreal situations**
>
> A **Imagine if** we <u>could</u> reduce our appetite for beef?
> B Some people **would rather** we <u>gave up</u> meat altogether.
> C It's **(high) time** we <u>started</u> exploring alternatives.
> D **What if** we <u>created</u> a cool new food product?

> **!** *It's time (that) we … = We should …*
> *It's high time (that) we … = It's urgent that we …*

Use the simple past for unreal situations …

1 to express present wishes and preferences. Sentence(s) _____
2 to speculate about or describe an imaginary situation. Sentence(s) _____
3 to express the need to do something. Sentence(s) _____

B ▶ Now go to page 137. Look at the grammar chart and do the grammar exercise for 10.1.

C PAIR WORK THINK CRITICALLY How would you like to see the world change? Write sentences using the expressions for simple past for unreal situations. Use the categories in the box to help you. Share your sentences in small groups. How likely are all your desired changes? Why?

> food   social media   transportation

Imagine if our school served gourmet meals! But honestly, I'd rather it offered more vegan options.

4 SPEAKING

A Look at the pictures of protein sources from around the world. Which ones are you familiar with? Do you like them? Would you like to try the others? Does their nutritional value influence your decision?

A Scorpion snack

B Fried silkworms

C Peanuts and grasshoppers

D Rare steak

E Seitan

F Vegan burrito

ACCIDENTAL STARTUPS

1   LANGUAGE IN CONTEXT

A   PAIR WORK   Look at the article title and headings and the pictures. What will the article be about? What other ideas might be presented in the article? Read and check your answers.

A LIGHTER **CARBON FOOTPRINT**

The need to find **carbon-neutral** sources of energy is a fact of life these days. The resistance to these efforts, primarily from multinational energy companies based on **fossil fuels**, is a fact of business. Stepping in to fill the gap are "social enterprises." It would appear that these community-minded initiatives, motivated by need rather than profit, are leading the way in our search for innovative, **renewable**, **low-carbon** solutions and becoming thriving businesses almost by accident. Here are a few of our favorites.

Solarkiosk

This startup has developed a kiosk with built-in **solar panels** that generate enough energy to charge batteries for everything from cell phones to appliances. The panels make it **self-sustainable**. Solarkiosk was designed as an energy resource for remote, **off-grid** locations. Though currently only in Ethiopia, Kenya, and Botswana, it is believed that this technology could be adapted for use almost anywhere.

Bio-Bean

Coffee already **energizes** us to start the day, but bio-bean has found a way to make it **power** more than our morning routines. This U.K.-based green energy company recycles coffee grounds into advanced **biofuels** and biochemicals that are more efficient than traditional ones. It would seem this company has found an affordable, **low-emission** energy source suitable for industrial-scale heating, among other uses.

Makani

This startup has come up with a renewable energy solution for island countries that have limited land. Their "energy kite" is a wind-propelled flying generator that flies in circles, gathering wind energy and turning it into electricity. It is reported that kites like these require 90 percent less construction material than conventional wind farms.

2   VOCABULARY: Discussing global energy issues

A   🔊 2.29   Look at the words and phrases related to energy from the article. Write *N* (noun), *V* (verb), or *A* (adjective) according to how they are used in the article. Listen and check. Which words have a positive or a negative connotation?

1 biofuel ___	5 fossil fuel ___	9 power ___
2 carbon footprint ___	6 low-carbon ___	10 renewable ___
3 carbon-neutral ___	7 low-emission ___	11 self-sustainable ___
4 energize ___	8 off-grid ___	12 solar panels ___

B   ▶   Now go to page 150. Do the vocabulary exercises for 10.2.

FIND IT

C   PAIR WORK   THINK CRITICALLY   Which forms of energy are the most common where you live? Why do you think that is? Use your phone to find out more if you can.

> We live in a very sunny place, but there aren't any solar panels anywhere! We still depend on fossil fuels.

3 GRAMMAR: *It* constructions

A   Look at the sentences in the grammar box. Then complete the rules below with the words in the box. Which sentences in the grammar box apply to each rule?

> ### *It* constructions
>
> A   **It would appear that** these initiatives are leading the way.
>
> B   **It is believed that** this technology could be adaptable for use almost anywhere.
>
> C   **It would seem** this company has found an affordable energy source.
>
> D   **It is reporte**d **that** kites like these require 90 percent less construction material.

> appear   report

1   *It* constructions in the passive are often used to _____ what people say or believe, especially in writing.   Sentences _____

2   To speculate about something or indicate that you aren't sure of the truth of the information, use the verbs _____ and *seem*.   Sentences _____

B   ▶ Now go to page 138. Look at the grammar chart and do the grammar exercise for 10.2.

C   PAIR WORK   Work together to report the information in the sentences using the verb in parentheses ( ). Then comment or speculate on the information. Check your accuracy.

1   Most people think that wind power is the cleanest energy source. (believe)

2   A lot of people like the idea that primary energy sources like coal will soon disappear. (hope)

3   Estimates indicate that many countries will have only renewable energy sources by 2050. (report)

4   Scientists believe that "waste products" like coffee grounds can continue to be useful. (think)

> ✔ **ACCURACY** CHECK
>
> Use linking verbs such as *seem* and *appear* after *It* + *would*. Don't use reporting verbs (*believe, claim, report, say, tell, think*, etc.).
>
> *It would ~~think~~ that solar power is a good option there.* ✗
> *It would seem that solar power is a good option there.* ✓

> Many social enterprises focus on providing **solar panels** or windmills because **it is believed that** these are the most **self-sustainable** options.

> Yes, **it would seem** wind energy is especially useful in coastal communities.

4 SPEAKING

A   PAIR WORK   THINK CRITICALLY   Which of the initiatives described in the text in exercise 1A would work well where you live? Why? How might they be modified to work better?

> People drink a lot of coffee around here, so **it would seem** that recycling coffee grounds is a good **low-carbon** option.

FIND IT

B   GROUP WORK   What other nature-based energy sources might work in your area? Use your phone if you can to do some research. Then report back to the class with your ideas.

> There is now a soccer ball that can catch and store energy as it moves. **It has been reported** that it can hold enough energy to **power** a light bulb for three hours!

10.3 A LIFE WITHOUT PLASTIC

LESSON OBJECTIVE
■ discuss the advantages of rethinking daily habits

1 LISTENING

A Look at the pictures. What are these things? What are they made of? What are they usually made of?

B 🔊 **2.30** **DISTINGUISH MAIN IDEAS FROM DETAILS**
Look at the points in the chart. Which do you think are main ideas, and which are details? Listen to Grace and Jake's conversation about adopting a plastic-free lifestyle and check your answers. Circle the ones you predicted correctly.

		Main idea	Detail
1	be mindful of your daily routine		
2	buy a reusable coffee cup		
3	avoid plastic straws		
4	how to live plastic-free		
5	recycle		
6	avoid over-packaging		
7	demand alternative containers		

INSIDER ENGLISH

It's doable = It will take some effort, but it's possible.

C PAIR WORK | THINK CRITICALLY Can you think of other everyday things that could be made of something besides plastic? Would they work as well? Why or why not?

2 PRONUNCIATION: Listening for sound changes in connected speech

A 🔊 **2.31** Listen to the sentences and match the underlined letters to the sound changes you hear.

1 But that talk really ma<u>de m</u>e want to try it. ___   a /d/ /j/ ——→ /dʒ/

2 How di<u>d y</u>ou start? ___   b /n/ ——→ /m/

3 There are lots of products out there that
  come <u>in p</u>lastic containers. ___   c /d/ ——→ /b/

B 🔊 **2.32** Circle the word that would cause a sound change when connected to the sound underlined. Listen and check.

1 Please don't use tha<u>t</u> *plastic* / *horrible* cup.

2 A recycling project needs very goo<u>d</u> *leadership* / *management*.

3 Was the presentatio<u>n</u> *planned* / *organized* in advance?

4 Coul<u>d</u> *we* / *you* try a little harder?

C Circle the correct words to complete the sentences.

In connected speech, words that end with /t/, /d/, or /n/ ¹*never* / *often* change if the following word starts with /p/, /b/, or /m/. Additionally, when a word ²*starts* / *ends* with /t/ or /d/ and the following word ³*starts* / *ends* with /j/, these sounds often combine to make /tʃ/ or /dʒ/.

3 SPEAKING SKILLS

A 🔊 **2.30** PAIR WORK **Listen to the conversation again and complete the expressions in the chart below.**

Defending an opinion and concluding a turn	
1 The speaker said that **it all** _____ being mindful of your daily routine.	C
2 **You** _____ **, but actually** … they're coated in plastic.	___
3 We can just recycle straws, too. **I mean, it's** _____ .	___
4 No, listen, **it's not as** _____ . I'm talking about …	___
5 It's too much all at once. **That's** _____ .	___
6 Anything that reduces plastic trash is worth doing. _____ **I'm trying to make.**	___
7 Recycling is only skimming the surface. **There's** _____ **that can be done.**	___
8 I hear you, **I just** _____ **anything so radical is necessary.** I think …	___
9 Well, **I guess we're going to have to** _____ on this.	___

B PAIR WORK **Look at the expressions in the chart again. Write *D* for those that indicate the speaker is defending an opinion. Write *C* for those that signal the speaker is concluding a turn. Compare answers with a partner.**

C PAIR WORK **Have a conversation about alternatives to other forms of plastic using the expressions from the chart above.**

> If everyone used crumpled paper instead of Styrofoam in shipping boxes, then packaging would be recyclable. I mean, it's not that difficult.

> It's not as simple as that. Styrofoam works better for fragile stuff.

4 PRONUNCIATION: Saying the /ŋ/ sound

A 🔊 **2.33** **Listen to some phrases containing the /ŋ/ sound. Repeat them.**

The first thing I did was buy a travel mug.   I'm talking about not using plastic at all.

B 🔊 **2.34** <u>Underline</u> **the /ŋ/ sounds in the following extracts and listen for them. Practice the conversation with a partner. Does your partner pronounce the sound clearly?**

A The speaker said that it all comes down to being "mindful of your daily routine"; that's when you notice things.

B I'm not sure going totally plastic-free is something people will respond to. It's too much all at once. That's all I'm saying.

A For me, anything that reduces plastic trash is worth doing.

B So, what other plastic things should we all give up, besides coffee cups and grocery bags, I mean?

C PAIR WORK **Complete the sentences with your own ideas and discuss them.**

1 You know something, I watched …   2 I'm going to start by recycling …   3 I think it's worth …

5 SPEAKING

A PAIR WORK THINK CRITICALLY **What are some other ways we might rethink the way we live daily life in order to be more eco-friendly? Consider the ideas in the box and come up with three or four more. Defend your opinions.**

appliances	a vegan diet	electric cars
importing food	walking	

B GROUP WORK **Join another pair of students and discuss your ideas. Defend your opinions.**

> It's crazy to buy cherries that have to come all the way from Australia when you can buy papayas that are grown right here.

WHAT'S YOURS IS MINE

1 READING

A Look at the picture of people using a ride-share service. Is this an example of the *gig economy* or the *sharing economy*? What's the difference? You can use your phone to help you. What's your opinion of these new economic models? Why?

B PREDICT CONTENT Look at the key words related to the discussion thread below. Which do you think will be used to defend new economic models and which to criticize them? Read the thread and check your answers.

> unfair competition   human-scale commerce   minimum wage

THE NEW ECONOMY: HAVE YOUR SAY!

Who are the real winners and losers in the gig economy? Is a sharing economy model any better? What do you think?

A ✗

Kevin
102 posts

When you read about the gig economy, it seems great for everybody, but let me tell you, there are losers in this story. Like taxi drivers. In some countries, it's very expensive to obtain a license – it's an investment. And once you get one, that's your job for life. Then ride-share companies come along, and because of the increased competition, they take away the taxi drivers' livelihood. It's unfair competition because it doesn't cost the other drivers much at all.

B

Amanda
58 posts

It's time that an economy based on everyone having regular, long-term jobs was challenged. The gig economy is all about on-demand services. Conditions might be more precarious for the worker – job security, insurance, benefits, etc., but we have to get used to that. It's the way the world is going.

C

Abdul
12 posts

What I like about the sharing economy is that it's a human-scale version of commerce, where you often meet the person who you're doing business with. Take Airbnb. That's a whole lot better than staying in an anonymous hotel somewhere. It's much more personal, and you get better service because of it.

D

Daniel
642 posts

The sharing economy is nothing new. Just look at libraries. We're just extending that model into the high-tech world. It's inevitable, like economic evolution. There's nothing we can do to stop it, so we might as well go with it.

E

Laura
21 posts

The "gig economy" business model revolves around tech companies that view legal regulations as outdated or irrelevant. They don't want to follow the rules, so they come up with a way to get around them. They still make money, but the people actually doing the work are NOT better off. In fact, the workers are all independent contractors rather than employees, so they don't get vacations or a minimum wage or sick pay or help saving for retirement. And what's worse, they can be fired without warning or explanation, so they can't even complain!

F

Carolina
33 posts

At first glance, I really liked the idea of opening up the economy. It's great for us customers, but I think a lot of people actually lose out. I mean, look at streaming music services. We save by not having to download music, but how much money do the musicians make once all the middlemen take their cut? And the food delivery apps! They take such a large cut that many restaurants can't afford to use them, so they lose customers they used to have. People need to understand that these cool new companies could be destroying small neighborhood businesses.

G

Sven
512 posts

Not so fast! In many places the gig economy has really benefited people, like places where there are no taxis, for example. Now people can use a ride service. How is that a bad thing? People can make extra money and learn new skills. I read that Uber offers English courses to their drivers because they know that it'll help them in their work.

C PAIR WORK EVALUATE INFORMATION Put a check (✓) for the contributors in favor of the new economic models and an X (✗) for those against them. Highlight the main idea in each comment.

D GROUP WORK THINK CRITICALLY Which of the opinions in the discussion thread do you agree with? Why? What could be the long-term effects of these new economic models?

2 WRITING

A Read the summary of the discussion thread. Does it focus on arguments for or against new economic models?

> The gig economy and sharing economy raise many different issues and opinions. The topic is **not at all** a simple one, but two clear arguments in favor of new economic models emerge from the discussion thread: freedom of choice and flexibility.
>
> Gig and sharing economy practices liberate people from the rigidity of a traditional working model, **so** it is beneficial to society. **In terms of** customers, they can have whatever they want when they want it – music, a place to stay, food delivery, a ride to the airport. **And for** workers, they are their own bosses, free to set their own hours and determine their income by working as much as they want. **In a nutshell**, the freedom and flexibility offered by these new ways of working make it beneficial to everyone.
>
> Though **probably true** that the gig/sharing economy is here to stay, **even if** we don't like it, the freedom and flexibility it offers has won it many champions.

B USE APPROPRIATE REGISTER Look at the **bold** expressions in the summary and their synonyms in the box below. Which set is more formal? Which expressions from the box could substitute for each expression in the summary?

by no means	in brief	in this respect
it would seem	regarding	regardless of whether
with respect to		

REGISTER CHECK

When writing a summary, establish up front that the opinions you're writing about are not your own and then write from that perspective. This avoids the constant repetition of phrases like *According to …* and *As stated by … .*

WRITE IT

C PLAN You're going to write a formal summary of the negative viewpoints expressed in the discussion thread. With a partner, look at the main ideas you identified in exercise 1C. What themes could you focus on in your summary?

D PAIR WORK Examine the structure of the summary of positive viewpoints in exercise 2A and discuss the questions.
- What is the role of each paragraph?
- How many points are presented in the body (middle) paragraph?

E PAIR WORK Work together to write your summary in 150–200 words. Use formal expressions like those in exercise 2B.

F GROUP WORK Share your summary with another pair of students and offer feedback. Is the register definitely more formal than the comments in the thread? Did they present all the main points? Did you organize your summaries around the same or different themes?

TIME TO SPEAK
Rent-a-Pet

A **DISCUSS** With a partner, look at the pictures of people and their pets. How do people usually get their pets? What's the best way?

B **PLAN** Form groups of three or four students. Half the groups are Group A, and the others are Group B. Read the instructions.

Group A: You want to start a business called Rent-a-Pet, a service that allows busy people to have a pet part-time. You must get town council approval. Come up with points in favor of the idea and take notes.

1 *Our business provides a home for rescue dogs and cats.*

2 *Busy people want pets but not all the responsibility of one.*

3 …

Group B: You are the town council. You approve or reject new business ideas like Rent-a-Pet, a service that allows busy people to have a pet part-time. Come up with points to explore and challenge this idea and take notes.

1 *Some pet renters might abuse or neglect the animal.*

2 *What if an animal bit or scratched the renter? Who would be responsible?*

3 …

C **PREPARE** Meet with one person from the other group to test your main points. Return to your group and share what you learned. Then prepare your presentation (Group A) or prepare a formal list of issues that must be addressed in order for Rent-a-Pet to get approval (Group B).

D **PRESENT** Carry out town council meetings with one Group A and one Group B. Each town council makes its own decision for or against Rent-a-Pet.

E **DECIDE** As a class, share the decisions of all the town councils. Did they all come to the same conclusion? What were some of the strongest arguments for Rent-a-Pet? What were the best arguments against it? In what way does this business idea fit the sharing economy model?

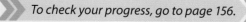

To check your progress, go to page 156.

USEFUL PHRASES

PREPARE

It's a kind and clever way to …

It's not as straightforward as that. …

The supply of animals in shelters … , but the supply of pet owners …

… That's all I'm saying.

PRESENT

We want to rethink the assumptions about pet ownership. First, …

Most people would rather … than …

But just think: What if we could … ?

From our perspective, it all comes down to …

UNIT OBJECTIVES

- discuss the importance of color for businesses
- talk about color expressions and their meaning
- respond to questions in different ways
- write a short opinion essay
- create a flag for a specific group

START SPEAKING

A   Look at the picture. Why do you think these people have painted their faces in this way? What do the colors represent? Have you ever done (or would you ever do) something like this? Why or why not?

B   Think of a group that you belong to. How do the members show their connection to the group (a song, posters, T-shirts, etc.)? What about other groups you belong to? Does the way you show connection change for different groups? Why or why not? For ideas, watch João's video.

EXPERT SPEAKER

What other examples can you think of to illustrate João's point?

THE COLOR COMPANY

1 LANGUAGE IN CONTEXT

A **What is the thing in the picture, and what is it used for? Have you ever used one? How many colors do you think it contains? Read the article and check your answers.**

Everyone knows the famous Pantone color swatches.

COLORS THAT WORK

Pantone, the world's number one color company, has a library containing 10,000 unique colors – from **bold** reds, **pastel** pinks, and **muted** greens to 71 different shades of white. The company has facilities around the world, and its products are used by 10 million designers and manufacturers every day.

Color has powerful associations. Any company knows that choosing the right combination of shades for logos and branding is crucial to success. For example, it's no surprise that gold and black **imply** luxury, but did you know that yellow **transmits** the idea of low cost? But which yellow exactly? Each shade **evokes** a different feeling. In this case, a **vibrant**, lemon yellow **conjures up** images of childish things (as all **saturated** colors tend to do), suggesting the product is cheaply made. If mixed with a **neutral** tone like gray, however, yellow **conveys** something more sophisticated. If neither of those yellows **resonate with** customers, they can easily choose one of the hundreds of other shades that Pantone has standardized with exact formulas.

Data also shows that Pantone has a big impact on the fashion industry. Every year, Pantone picks one shade that **reflects** current trends and **captures** the collective mood. News of Pantone's "Color of the Year" is anxiously awaited by designers. The next minute, it fills store windows everywhere!

B **PAIR WORK** **THINK CRITICALLY** **Do you think that the relationship between color and business success is as strong as the article suggests? Why or why not?**

2 VOCABULARY: Describing color associations

A 🔊 2.35 **Match the verbs in the box to the correct definition. Listen and check.**

| capture | conjure up | convey | evoke | imply | reflect | resonate with | transmit |

1 suggest _____
2 communicate beliefs, ideas, feelings, or knowledge _____ or _____
3 accurately represent something that is happening _____
4 have a particularly pleasing quality for someone _____
5 cause someone to remember or imagine _____ or _____
6 perfectly represent an idea or feeling _____

B 🔊 2.36 **PAIR WORK** **Listen to the adjectives that describe shades of colors and repeat them. Then find something around you or a picture on your phone that communicates each shade. Does your partner agree?**

| bold | muted | neutral | pastel | saturated | vibrant |

C ▶ **Now go to page 151. Do the vocabulary exercises for 11.1.**

D **PAIR WORK** **Find pictures of things in different colors for your partner to describe. What shade is it? What do the colors convey, in your opinion? Do they evoke anything special for you?**

> That couch is sort of a neutral tan color. It conveys feelings of calm and comfort to me.

3 GRAMMAR: Subject–verb agreement

A   **Look at the sentences in the grammar box, paying particular attention to the bold words. Then read the rules below and match them to a sentence in the grammar box.**

> **Subject–verb agreement**
>
> A   **Everyone knows** the famous Pantone color swatches.
> B   The **company has** facilities around the world.
> C   **News** of Pantone's "Color of the Year" **is** anxiously awaited.
> D   If **neither of those yellows resonate with** customers, they can choose another shade.
> E   **Data** also **shows** that Pantone has a big impact on the fashion industry.

1   Collective nouns (*group, company, team*) take a singular verb when the sentence is about the organization. When referring back to them, however, use plural pronouns.   Sentence _____

2   Singular nouns that end in *-s* (*news, politics, physics, economics*) take a singular verb.   Sentence _____

3   Some nouns that come from Latin form the plural with the ending *-a*. Some (*data, media*) take a singular verb, and others (*criteria, phenomena*) take a plural verb.   Sentence _____

4   Words beginning with the prefixes *every-, any-, some-,* and *no-* take a singular verb. Refer back to them with plural pronouns.   Sentence _____

5   Subjects with *either* or *neither* can take a singular or plural verb, depending on context. Refer back to them with plural pronouns.   Sentence _____

B   ▶ **Now go to page 138. Look at the grammar chart and do the grammar exercise for 11.1.**

FIND IT

C   PAIR WORK **Rephrase the sentences using the words in parentheses ( ) and check your accuracy. Then discuss the questions. Use your phone to help you find examples.**

1   We all have a favorite color, but is anyone's favorite color brown? What's your favorite color? (everybody / nobody)

2   Generally, the ocean is referred to as blue, but to my mother it looks green, and my father says it's gray. What do you think? (people / neither)

3   If you're going to a party with people you don't know well, you shouldn't wear colors that imply support for a particular political issue. Why do you think that is? Do you agree? (politics)

> ✔ **ACCURACY CHECK**
>
> **When the subject is *anyone / anywhere / anything*, don't use a negative form of the verb. Change it to *no one / nowhere / nothing* + a positive form.**
>
> *Does anybody like my idea for the new logo?* ✓
> *Anybody doesn't like* my idea. ✗
> *Nobody likes my idea.* ✓

4 SPEAKING

FIND IT

A   PAIR WORK   THINK CRITICALLY **Imagine you're talking to a graphic artist. Think of a popular brand and describe their logo and/or signature colors. What do you think of them? Use your phone to find pictures if you want.**

> IKEA's colors are the **saturated** blue and yellow of Sweden's flag, **transmitting** their identity as a Swedish company. For me, these colors **imply** bold simplicity, which **reflects** IKEA's style pretty well.

COLORFUL LANGUAGE

1 LANGUAGE IN CONTEXT

A **Look at the picture and read the quote. What do you think "out of the blue" means? (Answer is at the bottom of the page.) Do you have an expression for this idea in your language?**

B 🔊 **2.37** **Listen to Hyuk's report on color expressions. Do you have the same ones?**

"I hadn't heard from him in years, but yesterday he showed up at my door out of the blue!"

🔊 2.37 Audio script

My report is on the creative use of color in different languages.

Did you know that red is the color with the most common associations across cultures? When you **see red**, you get angry, and if you're **in the red**, then you owe money. In many languages you **turn red** when you're embarrassed, but only in English do you **cut through red tape** when you have to deal with lots of government rules and regulations. But don't cheat because people who get **caught red-handed** also get punished. (In Spanish, you *get caught with your hands in the dough*. I love that image!) So, red usually conjures up ideas of danger or negative consequences.

Green, on the other hand, is a positive color that evokes the spring, new life, and nature. In many languages, an ecological political group is called a **green party**, as in, "He's a green-party candidate for mayor." Someone like a gardener, who's very good with plants, has *einen grünen Daumen* – **a green thumb** – in German and English.

All you have to do is look at a traffic light to see that green means "go." And when you **get the green light**, it means you have permission to go ahead with a plan. So, green is generally positive, but color expressions aren't always black and white. Calling someone **green** or **a greenhorn** means they're too young and inexperienced to be taken seriously. And if you look **green around the gills**, then you probably don't feel well at all!

C 🔊 **2.37** [PAIR WORK] **Listen again and read. Find a color expression not related to green or red. What does it mean? Which color expression has two different meanings?**

2 VOCABULARY: Color expressions

A 🔊 **2.38** [PAIR WORK] **Use the categories in the box to group the color expressions in Hyuk's report. Some could go in more than one category. Listen and check.**

age	approval	bad behavior	emotion	government	health	money	nature

B [PAIR WORK] **Think about the expressions Hyuk mentions. To express the same idea in your language, would you use a color association or something else? How would you translate it into English?**

C ▶ **Now go to page 151. Do the vocabulary exercises for 11.2.**

D [PAIR WORK] [THINK CRITICALLY] **What associations does your culture have with red and green? What about other colors?**

> For us in China, red doesn't convey anger or danger, but good luck.

Answer: completely unexpected and surprisingly unusual, like a sudden lightning strike

3 GRAMMAR: Articles

A **Look at the sentences in the grammar box. Then complete the rules with the words in the box.**

> **Articles**
>
> Red is **the** color with **the** most common associations.
>
> People who get *caught red-handed* also get punished.
>
> Someone like **a** gardener, who is good with plants, has *a green thumb*.

    category   generalization   superlatives

1   Don't use an article when you're making a _____ .
2   Use the definite article (*the*) with _____ , with unique things, and to identify a specific noun that people share knowledge about.
3   Use an indefinite article (*a/an*) when the noun is first mentioned, not specifically identified, or part of a _____ .

B   ▶ **Now go to page 139. Look at the grammar chart and do the grammar exercise for 11.2.**

C   PAIR WORK **Complete the sentences about the color blue with *the*, *a*, *an*, or – (no article). Compare with a partner. Did you make the same choices?**

1   Her eyes were _____ same shade of blue as _____ sky and _____ sea.
2   Royal blue is too dark for this room. I prefer _____ lighter shade.
3   My daughter always paints _____ sky _____ purple in her pictures. To her, it just doesn't look _____ blue.

D   PAIR WORK **Choose another color and write three sentences about it on any topic. Trade papers and check your partner's work. Did they use articles correctly? Did you? Give each other feedback.**

4 SPEAKING

A   PAIR WORK **Look again at the color expressions in the report on page 110. Think of situations in which you might use one of them. Choose one of the situations and create a conversation.**

B   GROUP WORK **Act out your conversations with another pair of students. Did you all use articles correctly?**

I'm so angry **I'm seeing red**! I just bought this plant and it's already almost dead!

Poor thing. Give it to me. I have **a green thumb**. Maybe I can bring it back to life.

C   PAIR WORK **Think of color expressions in your language that use yellow, silver, pink, or orange. What do they mean? When are they used? Are there equivalents in English? For ideas, watch João's video.**

EXPERT SPEAKER

Do you have the same color associations as João?

11.3 IT TASTES LIKE GREEN!

1 LISTENING

A **PAIR WORK** Look at the different foods in the pictures. What do you think each food will taste like? Do you think they'll be sweet or savory? Why?

B 🔊 **2.39** **LISTEN FOR MAIN POINTS** Listen to a Q&A (question-and-answer) session after a presentation. Take notes on the main points that each speaker makes about the relationship between food and color.

Prof. Jenkins   People imagine different tastes based on color

C 🔊 **2.39** **PAIR WORK** **LISTEN FOR DETAILS** Listen again and write specific information about the topics below. Compare your work with a partner. Did you both note the same details?

- Expectations of taste and specific colors
- Color and the other senses
- Colored foods and marketing
- Cultural associations and food color

2 PRONUNCIATION: Listening for uncertainty

A 🔊 **2.40** Listen to the sentences from the Q&A session. Is the intonation of the <u>underlined</u> words the same or different? What does that tell you?

1 <u>Well</u>, that was fascinating.
2 <u>Well</u>, I'm afraid that's not really my area.

B 🔊 **2.41** Listen. Write *S* if the speaker is sure of what they're saying. Write *N* if they're not so sure.

1 That's a good question ___
2 Other results were interesting ___
3 Yes, they are ___
4 I see what you mean ___
5 I was just wondering ___
6 Yes, I can ___

C **PAIR WORK** Take turns reading the sentences to each other. Reply using intonation that shows whether you're sure of your response.

1 Most people have a lucky color.
2 Men and women have different perceptions of color.
3 Humans are unique in the animal world for appreciating color.

D Circle the correct words to complete the sentence.
The *fall-rise / rise-fall* intonation often means that there is something the speaker is unsure about or not fully prepared to state.

INSIDER ENGLISH

happen to + verb = coincidence
*"It could be another food that just **happens to look like** a chocolate cookie."*

3 SPEAKING SKILLS

A 🔊 **2.39** **PAIR WORK** Read the different responses to questions from the Q&A session. Match them to the correct function and write *A*, *B*, or *C*. Consider the context of the conversation to help you. Listen again if needed.

A Clarifying or asking for repetition   **B** Thinking aloud to formulate an answer   **C** Redirecting the question

Responding to questions

1 That's a good question … ___	**7** I'm afraid that's not really my area. ___
2 Would you like to take this one? ___	**8** Perhaps [*name*] can answer that one. ___
3 I guess I would have to say … ___	**9** Let me think … ___
4 I'm glad you asked that. ___	**10** Sorry, but what do you mean by that exactly? ___
5 Let me just check that I've understood your question. ___	**11** I'm not sure I understand. Could you rephrase the question, please? ___
6 Well, the short answer is yes / no. … ___	**12** Well, I've never really thought about it like that, but now that you ask, … ___

B **PAIR WORK** Think of some difficult questions related to color to ask your partner. Use the responses in the chart in exercise 3A in your answers.

> What colors are in the South African flag?

> I'm afraid that's not a country I'm familiar with.

4 PRONUNCIATION: Saying vowels before consonants

A 🔊 **2.42** Listen. Circle the word with the longer vowel sound. Are long vowels (like /iː/) longer before voiced consonants (like /d/) or unvoiced consonants (like /t/)?

1 a white	**2 a** green	**3 a** sweeten	**4 a** broad	**5 a** loose
b wide	**b** greet	**b** Sweden	**b** brought	**b** lose

B 🔊 **2.43** **PAIR WORK** Say the word pairs to each other. Write *S* for the shorter vowel sound and *L* for the longer vowel sound. Listen and check. Correct your pronunciation and practice them again.

1 a feed ___ **b** feet ___	**4 a** cause ___ **b** caught ___
2 a leaf ___ **b** leave ___	**5 a** route ___ **b** rude ___
3 a suit ___ **b** sued ___	**6 a** use (*n*) ___ **b** use (*v*) ___

C **PAIR WORK** Choose four word pairs from exercises 4A and 4B. Write a sentence for each pair but leave out the target word. Then swap papers and read one of the sentences aloud, including your guess for the missing word. Did you pronounce it clearly?

> Hmm. "There is a … *broad* range of colors in my son's toy box." Am I right? Is it *broad*?

5 SPEAKING

A **GROUP WORK** **THINK CRITICALLY** Discuss the questions.

- Think of a colorful dish or type of drink from your culture. Would a visitor be surprised by the flavor based on the color? Why or why not?
- If you could reinvent the item, how would you do it? Would your changes also change taste expectations? How?

> Fried green tomatoes are my grandma's specialty. They look like kiwi slices, but they're hot and salty.

> Would they taste good as a sweet dish?

A SENSE OF IDENTITY

1 READING

A   Look at the pictures of fans dressed in their team's colors. Which color scheme do you like most? Why? How important do you think a team's colors are? Why?

B   Where does each team come from? Which sport does the team play? Read the article and label the pictures with the team's name.

The fans win out

When you're talking sports, the importance of color cannot be overestimated. In 2012, Vincent Tan, the Malaysian chairman of Cardiff City soccer team in the U.K., decided to change the team's jerseys from blue to red because red represented good luck for him. At the same time, a dragon replaced the bluebird as the team's symbol. It turned out to be a huge mistake. Cardiff City had been playing in blue jerseys since 1908, and fans were not happy. After three years of uproar, Tan finally surrendered to tradition and changed it all back.

This story of fans embracing the iconography of their team's colors and symbols to give themselves a sense of identity and belonging is typical but not universal.

The Ecuadorian soccer team Barcelona de Guayaquil was founded in 1925 by Eutimio Pérez, a Spanish immigrant who named the club after his home city. They originally played in the characteristic blue and red striped jersey of Perez's beloved Barça team, but after a series of losses, the team president swore never to wear those colors again. In the 1940s, yellow was introduced and would eventually become the team's principal color, though the team still retains the crest, which is almost identical to that of the Spanish team in color and design. Thus, Barcelona de Guayaquil is a sort of hybrid – based on Barça but with its own colors and traditions.

In the United States and Canada, pro sports teams are privately owned, so it is not unusual for them to move when ownership changes hands. One team, however, is unique. The Green Bay Packers, an American football team from Wisconsin, is actually a non-profit, community-owned enterprise. The team's signature color, bay green, reflects the town's forested landscape and is a point of great pride for residents and Packers fans everywhere. It is unimaginable that the team would ever change its famous green and gold color scheme.

But that is by no means the norm. For a new or transplanted team, the owners usually choose a name and colors to reflect or honor their new home. For example, when the Pittsburgh Penguins ice hockey team was formed, it used the same black and yellow as the other teams in Pittsburgh – colors also on the city's flag. Some years ago, the Penguins changed the yellow to a true gold, but even that very subtle change displeased fans because the other teams in the city had kept yellow. So gold was out, and yellow was back in. As with Cardiff City, in the end, the fans won out!

C   **EVALUATE INFORMATION**   Read the article again. Take notes about the different stories related to the teams and their colors.

D   **PAIR WORK**   **THINK CRITICALLY**   Think of a sports team that you know something about. What is their nickname? What is their symbol or mascot? What are their colors? What do they represent for the fans? How are these things used in their uniforms and merchandise?

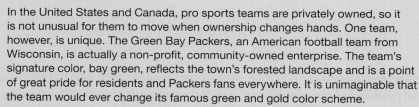

Real Madrid soccer team in Spain plays in all white. They are known as the "Meringues" because of this, but I don't know why they chose white.

2 WRITING

A **PAIR WORK** Read an essay on creating a new sports team and choosing its colors. What factors are discussed? Which one does the writer claim is the most important, and why?

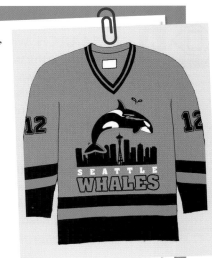

It is widely known that there is a strong connection between color and identity – schools, political parties, and sports teams all have signature colors. But what happens when you have to choose a name for a team as well as its colors?

Seattle, Washington, is set to get a new ice hockey team, and the debate over a name is heated. Many names have been proposed – The Whales, The Kraken (a mythological sea creature), The Emeralds, The Metropolitans – but there is no clear favorite among them. Seattle's other sports teams all refer to the town's history as a seaport: The Mariners (baseball) and The Seahawks (football). Some want to keep that tradition alive, but others think it's time for a change.

Though the debate rages on about the name and symbol, there is no disagreement on the team colors. Every proposal uses some version of the signature color scheme of the city's other teams. The distinctive dark blue / forest green / silver-gray combos mirror the landscape of the area and Puget Sound in particular – an inlet from the Pacific Ocean that surrounds the city of Seattle. This shows that color has more power to unite a group than symbols or even names.

B **SUPPORT OPINIONS** Read the essay again. What opinions does the writer offer? Note them below. What examples are given to support those opinions? Note them also.

1   color – identity connection   schools, political parties, teams

2   _____   _____

3   _____   _____

WRITE IT

C **PLAN** You're going to write an opinion essay of no more than 200 words. With a partner, look at the essay in exercise 2A again. How does the writer start the essay, with general or specific information? What is presented in the second paragraph? In the third paragraph? How does the writer end the essay?

D **PAIR WORK** Look at the two perspectives below. Think of possible groups you could write about and discuss the questions. You can use your phone to find examples to support your ideas.

Perspectives: It's time for a change. **OR** Traditions should be honored.

- How do the group's colors relate to the culture, geography, or history of the area?
- How much tradition is represented by the current colors?
- Would you like to see such a change? Why or why not? If so, how would you like to change it?

E **Working together, choose a perspective and write your essay. Use examples to support your opinions.**

Everyone in our country knows the national soccer team's colors. They are on the flag, in tourism ads, and in the costumes of our folk dancers. Recently, there has been discussion about changing …

F **GROUP WORK** In small groups, read your essays aloud and discuss them. Do the examples support the arguments? Do you agree or disagree with the writers? What examples can you give as a counterargument?

> **REGISTER** CHECK
>
> Use passive voice and *it* constructions to add variety and formality to an opinion piece.
>
> ~~Like most people, I believe …~~
>
> *It is widely believed …*
>
> ~~I considered several factors …~~
>
> *Several factors were considered …*

TIME TO SPEAK
Fly your flag

FIND IT

A   **RESEARCH**   With a partner, look at the two flags. Which one is the traditional flag of New Zealand, and which one was proposed as a new flag? What elements are the same? What's different? What do you think the new elements in the proposed design represent? If you can, use your phone to find out more.

B   The designers of the new flag proposed it because they wanted to better reflect New Zealand's national identity. What elements do you think they considered? Read the list and add at least three more.

Location: island in the South Pacific

Original people: Maori

National color: black

Biggest industry: sheep farming

History and current relationship with U.K.

_____

_____

C   **PLAN**   You and your partner are responsible for designing a new flag for an organization (your city, favorite sports team, a community group, etc.). What will the flag be for? Make a list of the elements you should consider.

D   **PREPARE**   Choose the three or four most important elements from your list to include in your design. Take notes about the reason for each element and give an example to help explain your ideas. If you can, create a visual of your flag to use in your presentation.

Flag for our school: should include quetzal – our national bird …

E   **PRACTICE**   Work with another pair and present your design ideas to each other. Offer suggestions for improvement and listen to their feedback. Then refine your design and your presentation as needed.

F   **PRESENT**   Present your design to the class, explaining why you chose the colors, symbols, etc., and answering any questions. Use visuals if you can to support your presentation. Which designs are the most interesting? Which one would win a referendum, do you think?

>> To check your progress, go to page 156. >>

USEFUL PHRASES

PLAN

If we make a flag for … , it should include …

The flag we make needs to evoke …

I think … is the most important element because …

The color … could symbolize both … and …

PRESENT

Our flag uses the colors … . These are colors that …

To most people, saturated colors convey … , but in our flag, …

That's a good question. … , would you like to take that one?

UNIT OBJECTIVES
■ answer job interview questions about change
■ talk about places that have changed drastically
■ tell a story that you heard from someone else
■ write a review of a movie or book
■ create a structured story from pictures

THINGS CHANGE

12

START SPEAKING

FIND IT

A   Look at the picture. What is happening? What type of animal is this? Why does it symbolize change? What other transformations occur in nature? Use your phone to find pictures.

B   Which of the milestones in the box do you think change a person's life the most? Why? Of those you have experienced, which has been the most challenging? For ideas, watch Susanne's video.

fall in love	get married
have children	leave home
lose someone you love	move to a new place
retire	start a new job
start school	

EXPERT SPEAKER

How has your experience been similar to Susanne's?

JOB CHANGE

1 LANGUAGE IN CONTEXT

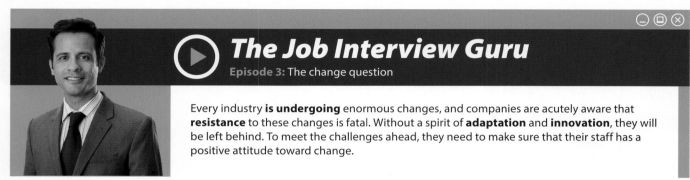

The Job Interview Guru
Episode 3: The change question

Every industry **is undergoing** enormous changes, and companies are acutely aware that **resistance** to these changes is fatal. Without a spirit of **adaptation** and **innovation**, they will be left behind. To meet the challenges ahead, they need to make sure that their staff has a positive attitude toward change.

A 🔊 **2.44** **Look at the screenshot from an online tutorial. What do you think the "change question" is? Listen and check.**

🔊 **2.44 Audio script**

Host	In this episode, we'll talk about the most important job interview question of all.
Guru	That's right. Companies today are insisting that recruiters find out as much as possible about a candidate's attitude towards change. The demand that employees be comfortable with handling change is universal, so I strongly recommend that everyone, no matter what the job, prepare a good answer to the question, "How do you handle change?"
Host	That seems like a simple question.
Guru	Yes, but your answer needs to show that you **embrace** change and see **disruption** as a chance to shine.
Host	And how do we do that?
Guru	An essential quality of a good answer is that it be practical and specific. Think of an example that clearly illustrates your positive reaction to change – a huge **shake-up** in your life, like a **transition** from one school to another, or a new management system that you **implemented** at work, maybe a policy change that you **facilitated**. Doesn't matter what. The important thing is that it shows you are not afraid of change, nor do you rush in with blind enthusiasm. So, you're aware of the **disruptive** potential of change, but you can evaluate situations objectively, then identify possible obstacles and come up with **innovative** strategies to overcome them.
Host	Sounds like a tall order! Let's look at a few examples. …

B 🔊 **2.44** **Listen again and read. Do you agree that a good answer to the change question is crucial to job interview success? Why or why not?**

INSIDER ENGLISH

a tall order = **a lot to ask**

2 VOCABULARY: Talking about change

A 🔊 **2.45** **Look at the bold words in the screenshot and the audio script. Make a chart like the one below and categorize the words according to how they are used. Listen and check. Which words suggest a negative attitude?**

Nouns	Verbs	Adjectives
resistance	undergo	

B ▶ **Now go to page 152. Do the vocabulary exercises for 12.1.**

C **PAIR WORK** | **THINK CRITICALLY** Read the expressions and discuss them. Do you agree with them? Why or why not? For ideas, watch Susanne's video.

Change is difficult; not changing is fatal.

The more things change, the more they stay the same.

If it isn't broken, don't fix it.

EXPERT SPEAKER

Do you agree with Susanne, or do you think it's good advice?

3 GRAMMAR: The present subjunctive

A **Look at the sentences in the grammar box. Then complete the rules below. Refer to exercise 1 on page 118 to help you.**

> ### The present subjunctive
>
> Companies today **are insisting that** recruiters **find out** as much as possible.
>
> **The demand that** employees **be comfortable with** handling change is universal.
>
> An **essential quality** of a good answer **is that** it **be** practical and specific.

1 Use the present subjunctive in *that* clauses after verbs that express a need to act, a request, or a proposal: *advise, ask, demand, _____ , order, _____ , request, suggest.*

2 Use the present subjunctive after nouns that express a strong request or proposal: *_____ , insistence, recommendation, suggestion.*

3 Use the present subjunctive after expressions containing adjectives that suggest importance: *crucial, _____ , imperative, _____ , vital.*

B ▶ **Now go to page 140. Look at the grammar chart and do the grammar exercise for 12.1.**

C **PAIR WORK** | **Look at the situations. Use the words in parentheses ( ) to offer advice using the present subjunctive. Check your accuracy.**

1 A friend is stressed out about an upcoming interview. (I suggest …)

2 A coworker had a heated discussion with his boss. (I recommend …)

3 You need people to understand an important rule. (It is essential …)

✓ **ACCURACY** CHECK

Be sure to use the base form of the verb in the present subjunctive.

I recommend that everybody ~~prepares~~ an answer. ✗
I recommend that everybody prepare an answer. ✓

The demand that we ~~are~~ on time was repeated many times. ✗
The demand that we be on time was repeated many times. ✓

4 SPEAKING

A **GROUP WORK** | **Look at the job interview questions below. As a group, prepare an answer to one of them. Remember, a good answer should be practical and specific. Try to use the vocabulary from exercise 2A in your answers.**

a Can you tell me about a time when you had to implement a change?

b What changes would you like to see being made in your current situation?

c What has been the most disruptive change in your life in the last 10 years?

B **Think of questions that interviewers might ask in different contexts. What advice would you give about answering them?**

> In a job interview, they might ask about past experience. I think **the most important thing is that you be honest** about what you find disruptive and what you embrace.

12.2 WHAT ON EARTH?

1 LANGUAGE IN CONTEXT

A Look at the pictures in the article. They show places that were once thriving communities. What do you think happened to them? Read the article. Were you correct?

INCREDIBLE SIGHTS AROUND THE WORLD
DRASTIC TRANSFORMATIONS ✈

Home   News   About   Sign out

San Juan Parangaricutiro, Mexico

Almost 70 years ago, this tiny village underwent a radical change. It was buried by the birth of a nearby volcano. The lava flowed over the whole village, leaving only the roof and the steeple of the cathedral uncovered. It's an amazing sight, emerging from the black volcanic rock that hardened all around it. Fortunately, no one was hurt. The lava is reported to have taken over a year to reach the village, so the villagers had plenty of time to escape. They eventually built a new San Juan, but of course, they would have preferred to stay in their ancestral homes.

The Aral Sea, Kazakhstan/Uzbekistan

The Aral Sea was once the fourth-largest saltwater lake in the world. More than half a century ago, this magnificent lake suffered a tragic transformation into a desert, with the dried-out bodies of old fishing boats dotted across its sandy landscape. Whole communities were forced to leave, sad to have lost their homes, their jobs, and their traditional way of life. But luckily, this drastic change was not a lasting change. In 2008, a dam was built for the purpose of redirecting water back to the lake, which seems to have worked. The sea has started to return, slowly but surely, marking a gradual but very welcome reversal. The people are moving back, too, glad to have lived to see their beloved Aral Sea come back to life.

Click to read more

2 VOCABULARY: Describing change

A 🔊 **2.46** Look at the adjectives in the box. Which are used in the article? Match them to the kind of change they describe. Listen and check. Then think of an example for each kind of change. Use a dictionary or your phone to help you.

INSIDER ENGLISH

slowly but surely = progressing steadily over a long time

abrupt	desired	drastic	fundamental	gradual
lasting	profound	radical	refreshing	subtle
sweeping	unforeseen	welcome		

1 a change described by its connection to time _____ , _____ , _____

2 a change that has a large effect _____ , _____ , _____ , _____ , _____

3 a small change _____

4 a change that people are happy to see _____ , _____ , _____

5 a change that was not expected _____

B ▶ Now go to page 152. Do the vocabulary exercises for 12.2.

C PAIR WORK THINK CRITICALLY Look again at the description of the Aral Sea. What do you think caused the transformation into a desert? Explain your ideas. Go online if you can to check your ideas and learn more.

FIND IT

FIND IT

3 GRAMMAR: Perfect infinitive

A Look at the sentences in the grammar box. Complete the rules below.

> **Perfect infinitive**
>
> The lava is reported **to have taken** over a year to reach the village.
>
> They would **have preferred** to stay in their ancestral homes.
>
> Whole communities were forced to leave, sad **to have lost** their homes.
>
> A dam was built for the purpose of redirecting water back to the lake, which seems **to have worked**.
>
> The people are moving back, too, glad **to have lived** to see their beloved Aral Sea come back to life.

The perfect infinitive is used to talk about situations and completed actions in the past.

1 It is formed with *to* + _____ + past participle. A modal is followed by *have* + past participle, without _____ .

2 It is used with adjectives such as *glad* and _____ and the verbs *appear* and _____ to comment on something that already happened.

3 It is used with reporting structures such as *it is said / thought /* _____ to indicate information is from other sources, not firsthand knowledge.

B ▶ Now go to page 140. Look at the grammar chart and do the grammar exercise for 12.2.

C Look at the pictures of Pripyat, Ukraine, on this page. What do you think happened there? Read the paragraph and complete it using the words in parentheses ( ) in the perfect infinitive. Were you right?

> ## PRIPYAT, UKRAINE
>
> In April of 1986, a reactor at the Chernobyl Nuclear Station exploded, contaminating a vast area and eventually killing thousands of people. Just three kilometers away, the 49,000 residents of Pripyat were smart [1]_____ (prepare) for this scenario, and their plan seems [2]_____ (work). The evacuation of the town is said [3]_____ (take) only three hours! More than 30 years later and still radioactive, the overgrown remains of the homes, offices, schools, and amusement parks are a ghostly reminder of what life might [4]_____ (be) like before the disaster.

4 SPEAKING

FIND IT

A GROUP WORK What other places do you know of that have gone through drastic or sweeping changes due to either natural causes or human activity? Discuss the questions. Then use your phone to find out more if you can.

■ What changes took place, and what caused them?

■ How were people affected by the changes?

■ Were the changes unforeseen or expected? Were the changes welcome?

■ Are the changes reversible? Why or why not?

B Tell the class about the places you discussed in your group. Which place changed the most drastically? Which change had the greatest effect on people?

> My grandparents' little seaside village has gone through a **profound** change. It's now an expensive tourism spot, so they had to leave. They were sad **to have lost** their home, but they were happy **to have sold** their house for a lot of money!

12.3 "AND THAT'S WHEN IT ALL CHANGED!"

1 LISTENING

A Look at the pictures of celebrity look-alikes. Who are they impersonating? Why do you think they do this? Have you ever seen a professional impersonator?

B 🔊 2.47 LISTEN FOR MAIN POINTS Listen to Talia and Maggy talking about a celebrity impersonator. Write short answers to the questions on the first line.

1 Who does he impersonate? _____

_____

2 How did he get into it? _____

_____

3 What was he doing before? _____

_____

4 What is he doing now? _____

_____

5 Is he happy with the change? _____

_____

C 🔊 2.47 PAIR WORK LISTEN FOR DETAILS Listen again and add details to each answer in exercise 1B on the second line. Compare with a partner. Did you capture the same details?

D 🔊 2.47 LISTEN FOR CERTAINTY Is Talia confident of the facts she's sharing? Why do you think that? Listen again if needed.

E GROUP WORK THINK CRITICALLY What happens to a story when it is told by a second and then maybe a third or fourth person? Think about a story you heard secondhand, or third- or fourth-hand. Would you call it gossip? Why or why not? What's the difference?

2 PRONUNCIATION: Listening for sound changes in colloquial speech

A 🔊 2.48 Listen. Write the full forms of the underlined words.

He's British, which is <u>kinda</u> freaky, <u>'cuz</u> when he's not impersonating Obama, he's got this really thick English accent.

1 _____   2 _____

B 🔊 2.49 Listen and count the number of words you hear in the colloquialisms. Compare with a partner. Listen again and write down the full sentences.

1 _6_ _Do you want to meet her?_   5 ___ _____

2 ___ _____   6 ___ _____

3 ___ _____   7 ___ _____

4 ___ _____   8 ___ _____

C Check (✓) the true statement(s). Correct any false information.

☐ 1 Any word can be shortened or changed if it is said in connected speech.

☐ 2 In informal writing, colloquialisms are often written as they sound.

3 SPEAKING SKILLS

A 🔊 2.47 **Complete the expressions in the chart from the conversation in exercise 1B. Put the headings from the box with the correct category. Listen again if needed.**

Skipping details   Referring to the original   Signaling a retelling

¹ _____ were his exact words, … In his own words, … That's ² _____ he said. I got it straight from the horse's ³ _____ .	To make a long story ⁴ _____ , … And the rest, as they ⁵ _____ , is history.	I can't tell it the way he does. I don't remember/know all the ⁶ _____ , but … I can't ⁷ _____ for him, but … It's much ⁸ _____ the way he tells it!

B 🔊 2.50 [PAIR WORK] **Maggy is now retelling the story that Talia told her to Kwan. Use expressions from the chart in exercise 3A to complete their conversation. Listen and check.**

Maggy Well, his name's Sam, and listen to this. He's a professional impersonator.

Kwan What? No way! Who does he impersonate?

Maggy Barack Obama! And he's really good at it, or that's ¹ _____ , anyway.

Kwan How'd she meet him?

Maggy Hmm, I don't know ² _____ , but it was through Gael somehow.

Kwan Oh, OK. So, he really looks like Barack Obama?

Maggy Talia says they could be twins. In fact, those ³ _____ : "They're like twins!"

4 PRONUNCIATION: Reading aloud

A 🔊 2.51 [PAIR WORK] **Listen to the information about Barack Obama and read along. Then practice reading it aloud to each other with the same stresses and word groups.**

<u>Barack Obama</u> was <u>born</u> in <u>1961</u>. // <u>Although</u> he was the <u>son</u> of an <u>American mother</u> and <u>Kenyan father</u>, // he was <u>raised mainly</u> in <u>Hawaii</u> // but <u>also</u> spent <u>periods abroad</u>. // <u>After graduating</u> from <u>Harvard University Law School</u>, // <u>Obama</u> had a <u>successful career</u> as a <u>lawyer</u>, // <u>showing</u> a <u>special interest</u> in <u>civil rights cases</u>.

B 🔊 2.52 [PAIR WORK] **Read more about Obama's life. Mark the word groups and stresses. Listen and check. Then practice reading it aloud to each other.**

Obama became president of the United States in 2008, having run a campaign based on the need for change and the importance of hope for the future. He was president for eight years, having successfully won reelection in 2012. Among his other achievements, Obama introduced a universal health care program and helped save the auto industry after a financial crisis.

FIND IT

C [GROUP WORK] **Write a similar paragraph about another influential person, but don't give their name. Use your phone to do research. Divide your text into word groups and mark stresses. Then, in small groups, read your paragraphs aloud and try to guess who the people are.**

5 SPEAKING

A ▶ [PAIR WORK] **Student A: Go to page 157. Student B: Go to page 158. Follow the instructions.**

"THE NEXT THING YOU KNOW, ... "

1 READING

A Look at the pictures on this page. What famous movies do they make you think of? Why do you think those particular movies were so successful?

B **READ FOR MAIN IDEA** Read the article. What does the author claim is the most important element of any screenplay? What movies does he refer to as examples for his arguments?

Turning points: the driving force of a screenplay *by Dean Martinez*

Fundamentally, all movies are about change: Someone embarks on a journey to discover the truth, solve a mystery, or learn about love, and they are never the same again. There are many ways to structure a movie plot, but the events tend to follow a three-act progression powered by key turning points.

In Act I, first we learn about normal life in our hero's world, whether that world is a mall in suburban Miami or a space station orbiting Mars. Next, we encounter the *motivator* – something that will push or pull our hero in an unforeseen direction, resulting in profound change or major disruption. The repeated invitations to Hogwarts force a hesitant Harry Potter out of his aunt's house and into an unforeseen magical existence. The discovery of a little green plant in WALL-E's lonely wasteland of trash prompts the arrival of EVE, and robot love is born. We then quickly reach the first major turning point: embracing the challenge. Harry is determined to uncover the truth of his own hidden history. WALL-E makes the abrupt decision to grab onto the spaceship and get EVE back. By choice or by force, our hero now has a mission.

Act II, which makes up most of the movie, begins with the hero rising to the challenge, fully focused on the goal that is now their life's purpose – or so they think. Just as they start to make progress, they encounter setbacks that show the challenge to have been greatly underestimated. The stakes get suddenly higher. The mission expands. It isn't enough that Dorothy and Toto overcome dangerous obstacles and successfully reach Oz. To see the Wizard, she has to kill a wicked witch! And here we find ourselves at the second turning point. The hero accepts the greater challenge, comes up with a plan, and fights the good fight to the end of Act II. There is a win or a loss, which leaves us at the final turning point – What will our hero do now?

Act III, resolution, and all questions are answered. In thrillers, these answers often involve a plot twist – *Who is trying to kill Tony Stark and steal Iron Man? Not who we thought it was. The real villain is revealed to be* – well, I won't give it away. But even with a surprise ending, we and our hero can at last make sense of events and make peace with the outcome. Unless there's a sequel …

Sources: storymaster.com; screencraft.org; www.movieoutline.com

C **PAIR WORK** **ANALYZE CONTENT** Read the article again and complete the chart below.

START	20–25%			70–80%		END
ACT I: Leaving "normal"		**ACT II:** ³ _____ and setbacks			**ACT III:** ⁷ _____	
Focus: the ¹ _____		**Part 1** **Focus:** rising to the challenge	**Part 2** **Focus:** fighting the ⁵ _____		**Focus:** making ⁸ _____ of events; plot twist	
	Turning point #1: Embracing the ² _____	**Turning point #2:** Higher ⁴ _____		**Turning point #3:** Win or ⁶ _____		

D **GROUP WORK** **THINK CRITICALLY** Are you convinced by the author's analysis? Think of a movie you all know well. Map it to the chart above. Does it follow the outline? Do you think it's possible to analyze all stories, not just movies, using this chart? Why or why not?

WRITING

A   Read the movie review. Does the reviewer like the movie? Why or why not? Have you seen it? If yes, do you agree with the reviewer?

This week's movie review: *A Star Is Born*   ⭘⭘⭘⭘⭘

This story is so good, they had to film it four times! And the fourth version is just as powerful and dramatic as any of its predecessors. Telling the age-old tale of the transformation from struggling artist to headliner, *A Star Is Born* follows the classic movie structure full of twists and turning points, ending with an inevitable dramatic climax. Ally (played by Lady Gaga) is a small-town singer/songwriter who is discovered by Jackson Maine (played by Bradley Cooper), a country/rock legend on the hunt for new talent. After seeing her perform, Jackson is captivated by Ally's voice and becomes both a mentor and a romantic interest, at once her idol and her biggest fan. As Ally's star rises, however, Jackson's career begins to fall, and the couple faces the inevitable challenges created by the dramatic transitions in their lives.

Some critics claim that the movie is too long and melodramatic. Others say that, while the beginning is enchanting and we are carried along by the romance, the second half is disappointing. Personally, I felt swept up in the amazing performances of both main actors right to the very last minute. *A Star Is Born* is definitely one not to miss!

B   **CREATE COHESION** Read the paragraph below. Then find the sentence in the review that combines these six simple sentences into one complex sentence. What grammatical changes were necessary?

A Star Is Born tells an age-old tale. It is a tale of transformation. A struggling artist is transformed into a headliner. It follows the classic movie structure. It has a series of twists and turning points. It ends with an inevitable dramatic climax.

C   How many other complex sentences are in the review? <u>Underline</u> them. Choose one and break it into three or more simple sentences. What grammatical changes are necessary?

D   PAIR WORK Read the paragraph about another movie. Rewrite it and combine information into complex sentences. Exchange papers with a partner. Did you combine information in the same way? Give and receive feedback on your paragraph. Revise as needed.

La La Land is a movie about two people. Mia (played by Emma Stone) and Sebastian (played by Ryan Gosling) live in Hollywood. Mia is a struggling actress. She likes old-style Hollywood movies. Sebastian is a struggling jazz pianist. He loves traditional jazz styles. They each have a lot of passion for their dream. This draws them together. They begin a romance.

> **REGISTER** CHECK
>
> Complex, multi-clause sentences are common in written language, especially in reviews of movies, shows, and books, where they condense a lot of descriptive detail into one sentence, giving the reader an overview of the work being reviewed before expressing a judgment of it.

▶ WRITE IT

E   PLAN You're going to write a review. With a partner, find a movie, TV show, or book that you both know well. Review the key plot points together but don't express your opinion about any of it. Then look at the review in exercise 2A again. Where does the writer give the key plot points? When do they express their own opinion?

F   Individually, write a review of the work you discussed in about 200 words. Use complex sentences to tell the plot and include your opinions.

G   PAIR WORK Exchange papers with your partner and read their review. Did you choose the same plot points to tell the story in your complex sentences? Do you have the same opinion of the work?

outstanding **unmissable** **edge-of-your-seat**
performance of a lifetime **action-packed** moving
dramatic climax **heartbreaking**

TIME TO SPEAK
Every picture tells a story

LESSON OBJECTIVE
- create a structured story from pictures

A   RESEARCH   In a small group, look at the pictures. What is happening in each one? What order should they go in? Could they go in another order? Rearrange them a few different ways. How does the story change each time?

B   DISCUSS   Use at least four of the pictures to create a story for a class creativity competition. As a group, first decide on the genre (romance, action, sci-fi, etc.) and the relationships between the characters. Then develop your plot.

C   PREPARE   Check your story against the chart on page 124. Does it follow the pattern? If not, does it flow logically? Does your story have a clear beginning, middle, and end? Does it include a plot twist of some kind?

D   You will have two minutes to present your story to the class, and everyone in your group must participate. Rehearse how you will tell your story and who will deliver which part. Try to maximize the impact of your presentation with clever timing.

E   PRESENT   Present your story to the class. Have fun!

F   AGREE   Vote on which story is the most creative. (You cannot vote for your own story!) Which story do you think would make the best movie? The best TV series? The best book? The best comic book? Why?

▷▷ To check your progress, go to page 156. ▷▷

USEFUL PHRASES

DISCUSS

Something terrible seems to have happened …

I guess it could have been …

If this one goes here, the plot twist could be …

PREPARE

It's important we be clear about …

Everything depends on … , so we should …

When you say "… ," then I'll step in and reveal the plot twist!

1 VOCABULARY

A (Circle) the best words to complete the conversation about how to market a food product.

A So, how do you think we should promote this new energy bar?

B Well, first we need to say that it's good for you. Mmm, it's nutritious and … it's ¹ *vibrant / wholesome*!

A Yes, that sounds good. And then we should say that the product is green, you know, it's been produced by means of ² *fossil-fuel / renewable* energy sources.

B Mmm, not sure we need to say that.

A I thought people want everything to be locally sourced with minimal ³ *carbon footprint / solar panels*. You know, like, eco-friendly.

B Yeah, but we can ⁴ *convey / imply* the message that it's 100% natural with the right image on the logo. Maybe a tree or a green landscape.

A Good! With some soft ⁵ *bold / pastel* shades, flowers maybe, to ⁶ *capture / conjure up* the countryside in people's minds. But there may not be room on the wrapper for all that.

B You know, I think the image should be more related to the ingredients, like ⁷ *appetite / foodstuffs* – you know, wheat fields or a close-up of some ⁸ *fiber / grains* of wheat.

A I think it should ⁹ *power / reflect* a natural, simple life. Like a farmhouse that's clearly ¹⁰ *off grid / low emission* and disconnected from urban life.

B Or maybe we shouldn't use an image at all – the wrapper is very small.

A So how about just a ¹¹ *muted / saturated* light green color with some leaves drawn on lightly? That would evoke nature and healthy eating, right?

B Great! We've got it!

B PAIR WORK **Think of a product that you know well. How is it marketed? What kinds of images and colors does it use? What do these evoke to you?**

2 GRAMMAR

A **Rewrite the sentences using the words in parentheses ( ).**

1 The time has come to paint the house. (high time)

_____

2 I would prefer us to stay in tonight. I'm really tired. (would rather)

_____

3 People believe that Pompeii is the greatest Roman ruin. (believed)

_____

4 News services have said that the prisoners escaped through a tunnel. (reported)

_____

5 The latest statistics show that unemployment is falling. (data)

_____

6 The headlines today are all about the train strike. (news)

_____

B PAIR WORK **Make sentences that are true for you using the words in parentheses ( ) in exercise 2A. Share them with your partner.**

> It's high time I started running again. My knee has felt fine for a while now.

3 VOCABULARY

A **Complete the essay on change with the correct form of the words in parentheses ( ).**

Big life changes are difficult but inevitable. Moving, for example, is said to be one of the most ¹_____ (disrupt) and stressful things a person can do. ²_____ (last) changes, like those that require ³_____ (adapt) to new surroundings, can lead to emotional distress, too. Even if the change is a ⁴_____ (desire) one, it's normal for people to feel some degree of ⁵_____ (resist).

My family ⁶_____ (undergo) a really ⁷_____ (sweep) change recently. My company developed this really ⁸_____ (innovate) software, which helped us get an important contract with a Canadian company, and my bosses put me in charge of it. That meant moving my family to Canada immediately. Talk about an ⁹_____ (abrupt) change! We weren't against the idea, but there are always lots of ¹⁰_____ (not foresee) problems to deal with. My company promised to do whatever they could to make the ¹¹_____ (transit) easier for us.

After the shock went away, we decided to see this huge change as ¹²_____ (refresh), a chance to learn about a new place and new culture. We've been in Canada two months now, and it's great!

B **PAIR WORK** **Do you agree with what the author says about change? Which changes are welcome for you, and which ones are disruptive? Why?**

4 GRAMMAR

A **Complete the sentences with words from the box in the correct form. You won't use all of them.**

be	bring	embrace	facilitate	meet
sell	shake-up	suggest	undergo	win

1 I suggest we _____ the changes they're making at the office and try to make the best of it all. This _____ is happening, whether we like it or not.

2 The tour company sent us an email. They recommend that we _____ clothes for all types of weather. The climate is unpredictable at this time of year.

3 The suggestion from the school board that classes _____ in the gym during the renovation has not been popular. No one wants to sit on the floor all day.

4 We were so lucky _____ tickets to that concert. No way could we have afforded to buy them, and the band broke up one month later!

B **PAIR WORK** **Make sentences of your own using the other words in the box. Read them to your partner. Give each other feedback.**

We were fortunate to have sold our house before the financial crisis started. Real estate prices have really dropped!

This page is intentionally left blank

GRAMMAR REFERENCE AND PRACTICE

7.1   NEGATIVE AND LIMITING ADVERBIALS (PAGE 67)

> **Negative and limiting adverbials**
>
> To add emphasis, you can start a sentence with a strong adverbial phrase. Negative adverbials include *Never, Never again, Never before, No way, Not until.* Limiting adverbials include *Little, Hardly, Only then, Only when.*
>
> **1** When a sentence starts with a negative or limiting adverbial, the word order in the verb phrase changes so that the auxiliary verb comes before the subject.
> _Never again_ **will I** *take my family for granted.*   _Only then_ **can we** *really understand our own history.*
> _Only when everyone is settled and paying attention_ **am I** *starting the presentation.*
>
> **2** When the verb is in the simple present or simple past, it expands to include the auxiliary verb *do/does* or *did.* This looks like question order, but the adverbial before it marks it as a statement.
> _Not until then_ **did** I fully **appreciate** *their importance.*   _Little_ **do** *they* **know** *what they're going to find.*

A   **Rewrite the sentences using the adverbial in parentheses ( ).**

1   I didn't think about the consequences until I got the results. (Not until)

2   We had only just arrived when someone knocked at the door. (Hardly)

3   I didn't tell anyone my news until I got home. (Only when)

4   This was the first time I'd come face to face with my grandfather. (Never before)

5   I didn't suspect there was so much more to the story. (Little)

6   We would never see my aunt's beautiful, smiling face again. (Never)

7.2   FRONTING ADVERBIALS (PAGE 69)

> **Fronting adverbials**
>
> To add dramatic effect, you can bring adverbials of place or movement to the front of a sentence.
>
> **1** When the subject of the sentence does not take a direct object, the **subject** and <u>verb</u> of the main clause change position. This is true when:
>
> - the verb is *be*   *In the envelopes* <u>are</u> **crisp new dollar bills.**
> - the verb indicates place, like *sit* or *lie*   *On the table cloth* <u>lies</u> **a stack of red envelopes.**
> - the verb indicates movement, like *fly* or *waft*   *From the kitchen* <u>wafts</u> **the smell of fresh dumplings.**
>
> **2** If the subject has a direct object, the word order does not change.
> *In the garden,* **she** <u>placed</u> a little ceramic frog *near the door for good luck.*

A   **Change the sentences so that they have fronting adverbials. More than one correct answer is possible.**

1   A soft breeze floats in through the window every morning.

2   Three generations of the Escobar family waited in the living room.

3   A small boy stands silently between the chairs.

4   The big tree we played in as children is next to the front door.

5   A cold wind blows under the door, warning us all of the coming winter.

8.1 PHRASES WITH *GET* (PAGE 77)

Phrases with *get*

The verb *get* is often used with other verbs to express causation, completion, and changing states.

1 To describe the completion of a task, use *get* + noun/pronoun + past participle.
   *How can I **get this paper finished** with all the noise you're making?*

2 To describe a changing state, use *get* + past participle.
   *In the second act, the story **gets very complicated** and hard to follow.*

3 To indicate that something or someone is prompting an action, use *get* + noun/pronoun + verb + *-ing*.
   *Coffee is the only thing that can **get me moving** in the morning.*

4 To indicate that something or someone else is responsible for an action, use *get* + noun/pronoun + past participle (+ *by* …). (Note: This is passive voice construction using *get* instead of *be*.)
   *Our new sofa **is getting delivered** (by the store) this afternoon.*

5 If someone or something else (not the subject) will cause a task to be done, we can use *get* or *have*.
   *We're going to **get**/**have** internet service installed on Tuesday.*

A **Write five sentences about your life using *get* in the five different ways presented in the chart. Which of your sentences can also use *have*?**

8.2 PHRASES WITH *AS* (PAGE 79)

A **Combine the sentences using a phrase with *as*. More than one correct answer is possible.**

1 We learned something in class. Most people can tell the difference between two nearly identical pictures instantly.

2 The majority of people say that they trust their gut about entertainment. Here is an example of that.

3 First impressions usually turn out to be wrong. That's what our survey results indicate.

4 We can all guess the answer. Is it better to marry someone you just met or get to know them first?

5 Fairy tales illustrate a lot of basic truths. For example, a person can fool you for a while, but not forever.

9.1 REFERENCING (PAGE 87)

Referencing

Referencing techniques make it possible to avoid repetition in a text.

1 To avoid repeating a noun or concept mentioned earlier in the same text, use …

- pronouns such as *it, they, them, this* (the pronoun *it* can also refer forward to a new idea)
- possessive adjectives such as *its* and *their*
- phrases such as *the same* or *similar* + noun

   *A sedentary lifestyle has harmful side effects. **It** increases the risk of cardiovascular disease.*
   ***It**'s worrying that young children are not getting enough exercise.*
   *Pedal desks help students focus on **their** studies.*
   *Schools give children active alternatives. Companies offer their workers **the same**.*

2 To avoid repeating a verb or verb phrase, use an auxiliary verb such as *be, have,* or *do*. Make sure the auxiliary verb is in the same form as the original verb.

   *The fact that a sedentary lifestyle is bad for you doesn't make for a big news story, but the fact that the sitting disease now affects all ages **does**.*
   *She doesn't like it, but her parents **do**.*
   *They haven't tried it, but he **has**.*

A **Complete the promotional announcement with appropriate referencing devices.**

Our sedentary lifestyle is killing us!

But engineers at Hamster Desks have come up with a solution.

¹ _____'s revolutionary and fun!

No more high cholesterol levels, chronic back pain, or early morning trips to the gym.
With ² _____ new office concept, you can exercise while you work.

Hamster wheel desks allow you to walk and work.
³ _____ save you time at the gym and keep you focused on work.

Do you want to maximize your time?
Well, there's no better way to ⁴ _____ it than with a Hamster Desk!

Be the first to get a Hamster Desk workstation for your office.
Soon all your coworkers will want the ⁵ _____ .

No doubt about it, ⁶ _____ ***is the best way to beat the sitting disease!***

9.2 CONTINUOUS INFINITIVES (PAGE 89)

Continuous infinitives

The continuous form of an infinitive verb emphasizes that an action is in progress over a period of time.

1   *to be* + verb + *-ing*
  - Use with the verbs *appear* and *seem* to comment on ongoing actions and situations.
  - Use with the verbs *want*, *would like*, and *need* to comment on intentions and plans.
    *We're going **to be looking** at the flip side.*
    *We seem **to be packing** way too much into our days.*
    *We know we need **to be racking up** at least seven hours of sleep a night.*
2   modal + *be* + verb + *-ing*
  - Use with the modals *should*, *could*, and *might* to criticize or speculate about an ongoing situation.
    *You're watching cat videos when you **should be sleeping**!*

A   **Rewrite the sentences using the words in parentheses ( ) and a continuous infinitive.**

1   It looks like my daughter is sleeping, but she isn't! (My daughter appears …)
2   It has been suggested that the problem is growing. (The problem seems …)
3   I should run five to ten miles every day if I want to compete in the marathon. (I need …)
4   I was scheduled to meet with my manager right now, but my train was late. (I should …)
5   It's possible that we may drive for 24 hours straight. (We …)

10.1 SIMPLE PAST FOR UNREAL SITUATIONS (PAGE 99)

Simple past for unreal situations

The simple past does not always refer to the past. When used with particular structures or in particular expressions, the simple past can be used to express hypothetical or desirable situations.

1   In unreal conditional sentences, use *if* + simple past.
    *If we **had** a more varied diet, we would reduce our negative effect on the environment.*
2   To express present wishes, desires, and preferences, use *I wish / If only / would rather* + simple past.
    ***I wish** / **If only** people **were** more careful about what they ate.*
    *My parents **would rather** we **didn't eat** red meat.*
3   To speculate or describe an imaginary situation, use *What if / Imagine (if) / Suppose* + simple past.
    ***What if** we **created** a new food product based on insect protein?*
    ***Imagine (if)** we **started** a company based on our new product!*
    ***Suppose** we all **stopped** eating beef. What would we eat instead?*
4   To make comparisons, use *as if / as though / even if* + simple past.
    *We cannot keep ignoring the problems **as if** / **as though** they **didn't exist**.*
    ***Even if** people **knew** all the benefits, it would still be hard to reduce meat consumption.*
5   To express the need to start doing something, use *It's (about / high) time (we)* + simple past.
    ***It's time** we **started** exploring alternatives. Let's make a list.*
    ***It's high time** we **expanded** our diet to include insect proteins.*

A   **Rewrite the sentences using the words in parentheses ( ) and an appropriate simple past expression.**

1   I don't like it that they're driving here. Public transportation is faster. (I'd rather)
2   A new apartment would be good. We've lived in this ugly place too long. (It's time)
3   Imagine living to be 120 years old. (What if)
4   Just imagine it: All people on earth are vegans, so climate change slows down enormously. (*if* + simple past)
5   I warned you that her dog bites. Stop acting like this is new information. (as if / though)

10.2 *IT* CONSTRUCTIONS (PAGE 101)

> ### *It* constructions
>
> *It* constructions make statements more impersonal and objective. They are common in academic writing.
>
> 1 To report ideas without stating the source, use *It* + passive reporting verb.
>   ***It is said*** *that renewable energy is our future.*
>   ***It has been argued*** *that climate change is the cause of the increase in hurricanes.*
>   ***It was found*** *that solar batteries can be adapted for use almost anywhere.*
>
> 2 When summarizing, speculating about, or drawing a conclusion about an idea, the choice of verb and adjective determines the degree of certainty and strength of the statement.
>   ■ *It* + *is* + adjective + infinitive   ***It is reasonable to assume*** *a connection between fossil fuels and climate change.*
>   ■ *It* + *is/appears/seems* + adjective + *that* clause
>   ***It seems unlikely that*** *social enterprises will replace traditional energy companies.*
>   ■ *It* + *appears/seems* + *that* clause   ***It appears that*** *this may be a solution to a lot of our problems.*
>   ■ *It* + modal + verb (+ noun / verb phrase) + *that* clause
>   ***It could be a mistake to assume that*** *this trend will continue.*
>   ■ *It* + modal + verb + adjective
>   ***It would seem logical*** *to start small, but a wider presence is necessary for success.*

A **Rewrite the sentences using an appropriate *It* construction.**

1 Everybody now believes that it's too late to stop global warming completely.
2 According to the research I've done, nobody has figured out how to recycle Styrofoam containers yet.
3 The newspapers have just reported that the government will give tax breaks to companies that use solar energy.
4 There is no indication that cell phone use will decrease in the future.
5 The general feeling is that the people in this neighborhood don't want to put windmills on their houses.

11.1 SUBJECT–VERB AGREEMENT (PAGE 109)

> ### Subject–verb agreement
>
> 1 Collective nouns take a singular verb when the focus is on the organization as a whole. They take a plural verb when the context clearly refers to the people in the organization. Some common examples: *association, class, club, community, department, family, government, press, public, school, staff*
>   *The marketing **department is located** on the third floor.*
>   *The marketing **department are** so excited to show everyone the new logo at the meeting.*
>
> 2 Singular nouns that end in *-s* take a singular verb. Some common examples: *gymnastics, news, politics.* School subjects that end in *-s* take a singular verb when they refer to a class or subject of study. Some common examples: *economics, ethics, mathematics, physics, statistics*
>   *Good **news is** always welcome.   **Economics starts** at 11, I have lunch, and then **physics is** at two.*
>
> 3 Some words that come from Latin (*datum, medium, criterion, phenomenon*) form the plural with the ending *-a*. Some (*media, data*) take a singular verb. Some (*criteria, phenomena*) take a plural verb.
>   *The **media** never **admits** when **they're** wrong about something.*
>   *His team documented **phenomena** that **show** that color can change behavior.*
>
> 4 Words beginning with the prefixes *every-, any-, some-,* and *no-* take a singular verb. When referring back to them, however, use plural pronouns *they, them,* or *their.*   ***Everyone knows*** *that red means stop.*
>   ***Nowhere is*** *the preference for blue more obvious than in the clothing industry.*
>
> 5 When the subject of a sentence or clause includes *either* or *neither*, the form of the verb depends on context. When referring back to them, however, use plural pronouns *they, them,* or *their.*
>   *If **neither of them cares** about the color, **they** should paint it white.* (not one person or the other person **cares**)
>   ***Either John or my parents** are going to meet us at the station.* (one person or two people **are**)
>
> 6 Monetary amounts take a singular verb when the focus is on the amount as one thing.
>   ***A thousand dollars is** a lot of money for one dress!*

A Complete the sentences with the correct form of the verb in parentheses ( ).

1 Everybody _____ (know) that a company like this _____ (make) a big profit.

2 I think statistics _____ (be) a difficult subject. The data on unemployment rates that I need for my project _____ (be) so confusing.

3 Neither the lawyer nor the paralegal _____ (have) time to see you now. They meet with new clients on Fridays.

4 The news today _____ (be) all about the elections in Mexico City. Politics _____ (be) often the focus at this time of year.

5 Nobody _____ (feel) good about this decision. The committee usually _____ (vote) one way or the other, but today they _____ (be) split five to four.

6 Please give! A few cents a day _____ (be) all that's needed to make a big difference.

11.2 ARTICLES (PAGE 111)

Articles

1 Use a definite article …
- when you both share knowledge of the noun.
  *In U.S. weddings, it is common for **the** bride to wear white.*
- when you are giving additional information to identify a specific noun previously mentioned.
  *Members of **a** team wear uniforms so people can identify **the** team on the field.*
- with superlatives.
  *This is **the** darkest shade of green I've ever seen in a living room.*
- to talk about things that are unique: *the king, the moon, the equator, the army, the media.*
  *People used to say that **the** moon was made of green cheese.*
- with general geographical areas: *the beach, the country, the town, the forest.*
  *This color scheme reminds me of **the** beach.*

2 Use no article when a non-count noun or plural noun is being used to make a generalization.
*Color can evoke **feelings** and **memories** just like **sound** can.*

3 Use an indefinite article …
- when the noun is first mentioned, new to the reader, or not specifically identified.
  *He used **a** shade of orange that I've never seen before.*
- to talk about jobs and professions or when the noun is part of a category.
  *I'm **a** real estate agent, but I'd like to work as **an** interior decorator one day.*
- when making a generalization using a singular noun.
  *Muted yellows and greens work really well in **an** open space, like **a** kitchen.*

A Complete the sentences with *a, an, the,* or – (no article).

Some people would argue that ¹_____ colors are not important in ²_____ daily life, but if, for example, you're ³_____ salesperson or work in ⁴_____ marketing, your image can be very important. If you dyed your hair ⁵_____ strange color one day, ⁶_____ clients might be turned off.

Consider also ⁷_____ colors you wear. Your clothes are ⁸_____ most visible thing about you and ⁹_____ first thing ¹⁰_____ people notice. ¹¹_____ colors you choose say a lot about you.

12.1 THE PRESENT SUBJUNCTIVE (PAGE 119)

The present subjunctive

The present subjunctive is used to lend authority to a speaker's words. It is usually used to refer to demands, suggestions, and recommendations; to describe what should happen; or to identify what is important.

1 Verbs in the present subjunctive do not add *-s* for the third person. The present subjunctive form of the verb *to be* is *be*.
   *He insists that we all **be** ready to go at noon.*   *I suggest that you **not come** any earlier than two.*

2 Use the present subjunctive with *that* clauses …
   - after verbs that express a request or a proposal: *advise, ask, demand, insist, recommend, suggest.*
     *He **recommended** that we **allow** extra time for traffic.*
   - after expressions containing adjectives that suggest importance: *essential, imperative, important, vital.*
     *It is **imperative** that he **complete** the application and **send** it in immediately.*
   - after nouns that express a strong request or a proposal: *demand, insistence, recommendation, suggestion.*
     *The officer's **demand** that we **pull** the car over and **wait** was surprising to all of us.*

A **Use the prompts to rewrite the sentences with the subjunctive.**

1 Students need to be on time for class. That's a requirement at this school.
   The school requires _____

2 He visits his grandma at least once a week, which they say is important for her recovery.
   For her recovery, it is important _____

3 The mayor has ordered people to stay indoors during the hurricane for their own safety.
   The mayor's order that _____

4 Medical professionals agree that all patients, whatever their age or physical condition, need to do some form of exercise every day.
   It is recommended that everyone _____

12.2 PERFECT INFINITIVE (PAGE 121)

Perfect infinitive

The perfect infinitive is used to talk about situations and completed actions in the past.

1 Use *to have* + past participle …
   - with reporting structures such as *it is said / thought / reported* to indicate information is from other sources, not firsthand knowledge.
     *The hanging gardens of Babylon **are thought to have been built** about 3,000 years ago.*
   - with adjectives to describe feelings that resulted from a situation or action in the past.
     *We were **relieved to have made** it to the end of the trail before sunset.*
   - with the verbs *appear* and *seem* to comment on something that already happened.
     *Based on the mess in the kitchen, her dinner party **appears to have happened** after all.*

2 Use modal + *have* + past participle with the modals *should, would, could,* and *might* to criticize or speculate about the past.
   *The residents **might not have wanted** to move, but they had to go.*

A **Tell the story behind the headline using your own ideas and perfect infinitives.**

MAYOR LOSES ELECTION AFTER CORRUPTION SCANDAL BREAKS

1 The mayor was shocked …   *The mayor was shocked to have lost the election.*

2 He thinks his defeat might …

3 In a recent newspaper story, he was alleged …

4 Sources say that the mayor is questioning the election's honesty. He is said …

5 Supporters of the opposing candidate believe the mayor should … .

VOCABULARY PRACTICE

7.1   TALKING ABOUT ANCESTRY (PAGE 66)

A   **Match the words in the box with the definitions.**

adoptive	ancestor	ancestry	ethnic	ethnicity
genealogy	genetic	heritage	inherit	

1   a person related to you who lived a long time ago   _____
2   belonging to or relating to genes   _____
3   the history and traditions of a particular group   _____
4   a person's family going back generations   _____
5   get from a parent   _____
6   related to a group of people with common origins   _____
7   the study of tracing a family tree back in time   _____
8   the group of people you identify with biologically   _____
9   taking in and accepting as family   _____

B   **Write the correct form of the word in parentheses ( ). Look at the chart on page 66 to help you.**

We were greeted at the door of the grand old house by an older gentleman. He was well dressed and friendly but walked with some difficulty. He invited us in and gave us a brief tour, sharing stories of his famous family as we looked at the many generations of portraits hanging on the walls. He was deeply proud of his
¹_____ (ancestor) home and clearly enjoyed showing it off.

A young man joined us, and the gentleman introduced him as his son. The son looked very different from his father. In fact, the ²_____ (heritage) qualities so obvious in the older man's face were nowhere in the son's. We must have been noticeably surprised because the two smiled and explained that the young man was
³_____ (adopt) from another country, far away.

"He's lucky," the gentleman said. "He'll ⁴_____ (heritage) this house, but not my bad knees!"

7.2 TALKING ABOUT CUSTOMS AND TRADITIONS (PAGE 68)

A   **Match the verbs with the phrases.**

1   mark / observe   _____   a   the fight between good and evil
2   honor / pay tribute to _____   b   a special day
3   signify / symbolize   _____   c   a special person or group of people

B   **Circle the correct words to complete the paragraph.**

The Indian celebration Diwali is called the festival of lights. To ¹*mark / signify* the occasion, families place lanterns outside their homes to ²*observe / symbolize* their fight against darkness. Colors are also an important part of the ³*rituals / significance*. People draw patterns called "rangoli" with colored sand or powders on the floor outside their door. The intricate patterns ⁴*observe / signify* the unity of humans and nature and welcome guests to the house. Diwali is a very special occasion, and families of Indian origin ⁵*honor / keep* the traditions alive all around the world.

8.1 TALKING ABOUT ATTENTION AND DISTRACTION (PAGE 76)

A **Circle the correct words to complete the conversation.**

A I'm sorry to ¹*concentrate on / interrupt* you, but I need your help.

B That's OK. I could use ²*a distraction / an interruption*. ³*I've been / I got* focused on this report all morning, and my eyes are crossing!

A Well, it's about Sam. He's kind of driving me crazy.

B Oh, no! What's he doing?

A Well, talking. Not to me – to himself. It's so ⁴*distracting / interrupting*. It's impossible to ⁵*be interrupted by / concentrate on* your work when there's someone constantly talking. It's hard enough to ⁶*avoid / get focused on* distractions around here.

B I'll talk to him. Maybe we can move his desk to that area by the lobby. Then he'll be the one getting ⁷*distracted / focused*.

B **Complete the sentences with the words and phrases in the box. Which of the sentences are true for you?**

avoid	concentration	focus on	get focused	interruptions	stay focused

1 I turn off my phone when I'm working in order to _____ on my work.

2 I can't get anything done when I work from home because of the constant _____ in my house: the telephone, my neighbors coming by, sirens from the ambulances, my kids fighting. It's impossible!

3 When I get distracted by something, it's really hard for me to _____ again.

4 Sometimes you just can't _____ distractions. It's hard to be disciplined all day!

5 I don't think my powers of _____ are weaker now. If anything, they're getting stronger!

6 I'm not bad at multitasking, but I prefer to _____ one thing at a time.

8.2 EXPRESSIONS WITH *GET* (PAGE 78)

A **Look at the expressions with *get* in context. Then match them to the definitions.**

1 What are you **getting at**? I don't understand your point.   _g_

2 I've **gotten** really **attached to** my old car over the years. ___

3 I **got** really **frustrated** in line at the bank. They take so long! ___

4 It took him three tries to put the shelves together, but he finally **got** it **right**. ___

5 We need to **get rid of** that sofa. It's disgusting. ___

6 We **got the go-ahead** from the boss to hire the crew and get construction started. ___

7 I don't think I could ever **get accustomed to** driving on the left. ___

8 I just **got blown away by** how much damage there was. Would we ever get it all repaired? ___

9 Designing a computer program can **get** really **complicated**, so you have to stay focused. ___

10 It's easy to **get lost** on these trails if you don't pay attention to the markers. ___

11 We need to **get something straight**. This is my car, and I'll say who can drive it. ___

a figure out / understand

b feel close to or affectionately about

c be amazed / overwhelmed

d become familiar / comfortable with

e not know your way

f become difficult

g try to communicate

h receive approval

i feel angry or annoyed

j be clear about

k remove forever

B Replace the <u>underlined</u> expressions with a *get* expression. Make any changes necessary to the structure of the sentences.

1 When children are learning to ride a bike, they rarely <u>figure it out</u> immediately.
2 I can't understand what you're <u>trying to say</u>.
3 I <u>was totally amazed</u> by the news. I just couldn't believe it.
4 The campus was so big that I <u>couldn't figure out which way to go</u> while trying to find my classroom the first time.
5 It takes a while to <u>familiarize yourself</u> to life in a new country.

9.1 DISCUSSING HEALTH ISSUES (PAGE 86)

A Match six of the terms from the box to the correct descriptions.

blood pressure	cardiovascular disease	cholesterol levels	chronic pain
circulation	digestion	immune system	internal organs
joints	posture	sedentary lifestyle	side effects

1 what gives the body resistance to infection and toxins _____
2 the amount of a type of fatty substance in the blood _____
3 what you have if you spend most of your time sitting down _____
4 the position of the body when standing or sitting _____
5 medical conditions that affect the heart _____
6 the process of absorbing nutrients from food _____

B Use the other words in the box in exercise A to complete the paragraph.

Research suggests that standing for too long may also have harmful medical [1] _____ . It has been suggested that prolonged standing might cause [2] _____ in the hip [3] _____ and lower back, as well as affecting [4] _____ in the legs and feet. Although standing helps relieve pressure on your [5] _____ _____ , such as the stomach, liver, and pancreas, it has no effect on your [6] _____ _____ or general heart health. It is important not to stay still in one place for too long, whether you're sitting or standing.

9.2 DISCUSSING (LACK OF) SLEEP (PAGE 88)

A Match the phrasal verbs to their definitions.

1 eliminate *d*
2 go away unnoticed ___
3 slowly relax ___
4 accumulate ___
5 increase over time ___
6 reduce the amount ___
7 gently fall asleep ___
8 make time for an activity ___
9 obtain or achieve to reach a target ___
10 stop someone from going to sleep ___
11 motivate someone to do something ___
12 do a lot of things in a limited amount of time ___

a add up
b build up
c cut back on
d cut out
e drift off
f drive somebody to
g fit something into
h keep somebody up
i pack something into
j rack up
k slip away
l wind down

B **Complete the paragraph with phrasal verbs. Look back at exercise A on page 149 to help you.**

There's no doubt that ¹_____ _____ on screen time before bed and
²_____ _____ caffeine in the afternoon can help you get to sleep quicker, but there's
another problem. We ³_____ so much _____ our schedules during the week that no
matter how hard we try, we just can't ⁴_____ _____ the recommended number of
hours of sleep. Work commitments ⁵_____ us _____ late at night. Family commitments
get us up extra early in the morning. Slowly but surely, sleep deprivation ⁶_____ _____
until we're barely functioning by Friday.

But there's good news! Some research shows that by sleeping late on the weekend we can actually make
up for all those lost hours. Don't set you alarm clock Saturday morning – let yourself ⁷_____
_____ and take it easy. Feel the tension and tiredness ⁸_____ _____ .
All that extra sleep will ⁹_____ _____ to give you a cheerful Monday morning!

10.1 DISCUSSING GLOBAL FOOD ISSUES (PAGE 98)

A **Write the words from the box next to their definitions. There are three extra words.**

appetite	cattle	cereal	consumption	fiber	foodstuffs	grain
livestock	nutritious	shortage	superfood	supply	wholesome	

1 animals that are kept on a farm   _livestock_
2 cows that are used for beef   _____
3 anything people can eat as food   _____
4 a substance in certain foods that
   helps digestion   _____
5 wheat, corn, rice, oats   _____
6 able to improve your health   _____

7 a situation when there is
   not enough of something   _____
8 seeds used to make bread   _____
9 the desire to eat food   _____
10 how much of something
   that is available to use   _____

B **Complete the story with words from the box in exercise A.**

The açai fruit comes from a palm tree in the Amazon rainforest and has long been popular in Brazil. Now, however,
açai is gaining popularity in North America, not only for its flavor, but because it's ¹_____ and
²_____ . It's a great source of dietary ³_____ , keeping the digestive system clean and
functioning normally. It is also said to improve skin, boost energy, and increase mental function. For these reasons,
⁴_____ of açai has gone up dramatically around the world. People love it!

Try açai for yourself and you'll soon understand why it's being celebrated as the ⁵_____ of tomorrow!

10.2 DISCUSSING GLOBAL ENERGY ISSUES (PAGE 100)

A **Complete the story about a social enterprise with words from the box. There are four extra words.**

biofuel	carbon footprint	carbon-neutral	energize	fossil fuel	low-carbon
low-emission	off-grid	power	renewable	self-sustainable	solar panels

Pollinate Energy (PE) is an Australian social enterprise that is improving the lives of India's urban poor by
providing them with ¹_____ energy options. Cooking appliances powered by ²_____
_____ is just one way PE has helped families who live in ³_____-_____
communities and lack access to conventional energy sources. PE provides families with products that can
⁴_____ their homes but that are ⁵_____-_____ because they require
only sunlight or wind. If another energy source is needed, PE products are made to use only ⁶_____-
_____ or, better still, ⁷_____-_____ fuels, as opposed to the different
types of ⁸_____ _____ previously used in these communities.

B **Circle the best words to complete the sentences.**

1 Social enterprises have the knock-on effect of *energizing / powering* inventors to develop more creative ways to meet people's needs, help the planet, and also make a profit.

2 A *biofuel / fossil fuel* is produced through biological processes, such as agriculture.

3 Livestock farms are bad for the environment due to their *emission / power* of dangerous greenhouse gases.

4 *A carbon footprint / Low-carbon energy* refers to the total emissions caused by an individual, event, organization, or product. The smaller, the better!

11.1 DESCRIBING COLOR ASSOCIATIONS (PAGE 108)

A **Replace the <u>underlined</u> words with a verb from the box in the correct form. More than one option may be correct.**

capture	conjure up	convey	evoke
imply	reflect	resonate with	transmit

1 The strong colors and sharp angles <u>suggest</u> that the artist didn't like the person he was painting.

2 To me, this photograph of an eagle in flight <u>perfectly represents</u> the idea of freedom.

3 The child in the wagon, the ice-cream truck, the women wearing hats – it all <u>communicates</u> a real feeling of nostalgia.

4 I really love her paintings. I grew up near the ocean in western Canada, so her smoky greens and grayish blues really <u>are meaningful to</u> me at a deep level.

5 Looking at old family photos <u>brings back</u> memories of winter nights by the fire with my grandmother.

6 These new designs <u>show</u> the current popularity of pink!

B **Match the descriptions of shades to their definitions.**

bold	muted	neutral	pastel	saturated	vibrant

1 not bright, mixed with gray _____

2 bright and strong _____

3 not strongly any definite color _____

4 pale and soft _____

5 pure, not mixed with other colors _____

6 strong and noticeable against other colors _____

11.2 COLOR EXPRESSIONS (PAGE 110)

A **Circle the correct color to complete the expressions.**

1 My boss gave me the *green / red* light to go ahead with the project.

2 The police caught the burglar *green- / red-* handed as he was leaving the bank carrying a bag full of money!

3 I'm going to vote for the *green / red* party in the next election because they're the only ones with a focus on the environment.

4 Is she OK? She looks a little *green / red* around the gills.

5 I'm worried about my business. We've been in the *green / red* for about three months, and one of our clients just canceled a big order.

B **Rewrite the sentences using an appropriate color expression.**

1 You wouldn't believe all the official paperwork I had to do to open a business in a residential building!

2 Look at this garden! She really knows how to grow plants.

3 I can always tell when my little brother is embarrassed because his face changes color.

4 I'm not sure he's ready for the job. He's still a little young and inexperienced to handle so much responsibility.

5 She shouldn't watch the news. She just gets incredibly angry and is no fun the rest of the evening.

FIND IT

12.1 TALKING ABOUT CHANGE (PAGE 118)

A Make a word family chart for the words in the box with noun, verb, and adjective forms. Not all words have all forms. Compare your chart with a partner. Use a dictionary or your phone to check your work.

innovation	disruption	implement	embrace	innovative	disruptive
adaptation	resistance	shake-up	facilitate	transition	

B Circle the correct words to complete the answer to "the change question" discussed in the unit.

How do you handle change?

I enjoy working in ¹*a shaken up / an innovative* environment, so I generally ²*disrupt / embrace* change and see it as an opportunity rather than a threat. Recently, my team ³*implemented / transitioned* a new communication system across the company. I was chosen to be on the team that ⁴*facilitated / underwent* this massive ⁵*innovation / transition* because I helped choose it. Well, people didn't like the system at first and showed a lot of ⁶*embrace / resistance* to it because they feared that ⁷*adapting / undergoing* changes like this during our busiest season was too ⁸*disruptive / resistant*. But we went slowly so that it didn't feel like a big ⁹*facilitation / shake-up*. And after a few ¹⁰*adaptations / innovations* to align it with our company's processes, people really like it.

Do you think this is a good answer? Why or why not?

12.2 DESCRIBING CHANGE (PAGE 120)

A Write the type of change described in the examples. More than one correct answer is possible. Discuss your choices with a partner.

abrupt	desired	drastic	fundamental	gradual
lasting	profound	radical	refreshing	subtle
sweeping	unforeseen	welcome		

1 It was a beautiful day. The sky was blue, and the birds were singing. Then, all of a sudden, big black clouds filled the sky, and it started to pour down rain.

2 We hadn't expected the storm, but the cool water was actually really nice after the blistering heat of the sun.

3 Recent storms have caused a great deal of damage to roads and buildings. Many families have lost their homes, too.

4 They've caused the landscape to change also. When you look at photos from a hundred years ago, for example, you can see that some features are definitely different now.

5 No one predicted the negative effect the storms would have on the local birdlife.

6 Many species have disappeared from the local woods and might not ever come back.

B Circle the correct words to complete the sentences.

1 My mom made tacos for dinner last night. It was a *refreshing / sweeping* change from what she usually makes.

2 If you raise your chair a centimeter or two, you won't put so much stress on your wrists and shoulders. Sometimes just a *drastic / subtle* change in positioning can make a big difference.

3 This isn't working! We need to make some *fundamental / unforeseen* changes to the way we do our marketing.

4 He seems to have transformed over the summer. He grew his hair out, got a tattoo, and made a *desired / radical* change in his wardrobe. I didn't even recognize him at first.

PROGRESS CHECK

Can you do these things? Check (✓) what you can do. Then write your answers in your notebook.

Now I can …

☐ talk about ancestry and genealogy.

☐ use negative and limiting adverbials for emphasis.

☐ discuss cultural celebrations and preserving them.

☐ use fronting adverbials to add dramatic effect.

☐ share an anecdote about traveling and also comment on it.

☐ summarize a topic with information from different sources.

Prove it

Write down five terms related to ancestry. Use them to write a few sentences about your family history.

Rewrite the sentence starting with *no way*, *never*, and *little*: I thought her presentation would be boring, but it was interesting.

Write four verb–noun collocations associated with customs and traditions (mark an occasion, e.g.). Use them to write about a tradition that you observe.

Describe the look of a celebration with fronting adverbial phrases. For example, "*Around the fence* hang strings of colored lights."

Write a short conversation about a recent trip. Comment on your own story and respond to it.

Look at your paragraph from lesson 7.4. Find three ways to make it better.

UNIT 7

Now I can …

☐ talk about attention and distraction.

☐ practice causative structures with *get* and *have*.

☐ use *get* expressions to talk about actions and reactions.

☐ refer to information with *as* phrases.

☐ describe selling points and best features of products.

☐ create effective presentation slides.

Prove it

Write five phrases related to attention. Use them to write about an experience in which your concentration was tested.

Write four sentences using expressions with *get* + verb. Could you also use *have* + verb?

Write five expressions with *get*. Use them to write how you feel about the digital age. For example, "I *get frustrated* when …"

Why do we use phrases with *as*? Give three examples.

Think of an app and write a few ways to present its best features and main selling points, and then its specific selling points.

Look at your slides from lesson 8.4. Find three ways to make them better.

UNIT 8

Now I can …

☐ discuss health issues.

☐ use referencing techniques to avoid repetition.

☐ use complex phrasal verbs.

☐ talk about actions over a period of time with continuous infinitives.

☐ ask questions and buy time when answering them.

☐ explain how an initiative works.

Prove it

Write about three physical effects of some aspect of modern life on health.

Using different types of referencing, write a paragraph based on your sentences from the previous task.

Write sentences using the phrasal verbs *cut back on*, *drift off*, *pack something into*, *fit something into*, and *wind down*.

Complete the sentence using the continuous infinitive: "My career _____ nowhere, but I don't know what to do about it."

Imagine that you want to press a local government official on an important issue. Write three probing questions you could ask.

Look at your paragraph from lesson 9.4. Find three ways to make it better.

UNIT 9

PROGRESS CHECK

Can you do these things? Check (✓) what you can do. Then write your answers in your notebook.

UNIT 10

Now I can …	Prove it
☐ talk about rethinking issues around food production.	Write five words associated with food production and use them to talk about foods that are popular where you live.
☐ use the simple past to imagine possibilities or pose scenarios.	Complete the sentence about something wished for: Some people _____ we _____ _____ plastic at all.
☐ talk about rethinking energy options for the future.	Write five expressions related to energy issues: two with a negative connotation and three with a positive connotation.
☐ use *it* constructions to present information.	Write three sentences on topical issues or trends using *it* constructions. For example, "*It would appear* that beards are back in fashion."
☐ defend my opinion and allow others to give theirs.	Write a short conversation about using plastic. Use expressions to defend an opinion and conclude a speaking turn.
☐ write a summary of one side of a debate.	Look at your summary from lesson 10.4. Find three ways to make it better.

UNIT 11

Now I can …	Prove it
☐ talk about what colors represent.	Think of one color you like and one you dislike. What does each represent for you? Use different verbs in your answer.
☐ make sure different types of subjects agree with their verbs.	Do the nouns usually take a singular (S) or plural (P) verb? *company* _S_ , *data* ___ , *everyone* ___ , *criteria* ___ , *news* ___
☐ talk about color idioms.	Write three color idioms that you learned in this unit. Use them in a sentence in an appropriate context.
☐ use articles correctly in different contexts.	Write about your favorite color as a child. Do you still like it? Use *a*, *an*, and *the* correctly.
☐ respond to questions in different ways for different purposes.	Write one sentence to buy time while thinking, one to pass the question to someone else, and one to clarify your understanding.
☐ write an opinion essay.	Look at your essay from lesson 11.4. Find three ways to make it better.

UNIT 12

Now I can …	Prove it
☐ discuss change and my experience with it.	Think of two nouns, verbs, and adjectives related to the action of changing. Use them to write about changes in your life.
☐ use the subjunctive to present a call to action or important information.	Rephrase the statements as advice using the subjunctive: 1 Be adaptable. 2 Companies want open-minded people.
☐ talk about different types of changes.	Write five adjectives that combine with *change* and describe a situation that captures each one of them.
☐ use the perfect infinitive to talk about completed actions in the past.	Write three sentences about a change in the past using the perfect infinitive – with a modal verb, a reporting verb, and an adjective.
☐ retell a story.	Write a conversation about a story you heard from someone else. Use expressions to signal retelling, to refer to the original story, and to skip details.
☐ write a review.	Look at your review from lesson 12.4. Find three ways to make it better.

7.4 EXERCISE 2C STUDENT A

Read one perspective on the value of writing things by hand, and take notes.

A recent study claims that writing notes by hand helps us process and retain more information than typing notes on a keyboard. Researchers at Princeton University and UCLA conducted tests on students. Half were asked to take notes by hand as they watched a TED talk, while the others took notes on a laptop. All answered factual follow-up questions well, but the hand writers were significantly better at answering abstract questions.

The researchers argue that writing by hand forces students to process and synthesize the material, as they can't write down every word. Typers could record more information, but they did not retain it as well.

12.3 EXERCISE 5A STUDENT A

1 **Read a story about how life changed in an instant.**

Leila's story

I used to be afraid of flying. I mean, terrified. Then my best friend asked me to be in her wedding – in Australia! So, no choice, I had to get on a plane.

Waiting at the gate, I was feeling very nervous. Someone said it was going to be a really rough flight – bad weather or something. Great! I was taking deep breaths, trying to calm myself, when I noticed this old guy a few meters away also breathing deeply. He looked even more scared than me, and for some reason that made me feel calmer.

We boarded the plane, and his seat was near mine. I swapped with the person next to him and sat down. I introduced myself and told him that I'd seen him before and how his fear had actually lessened mine, so I thought maybe we could get through this experience together. He was all for it. We talked all through the flight, which was horrible, by the way. There was so much turbulence! We just gripped the armrests and kept talking.

We said goodbye at baggage claim, and I said I hoped his flight home was better than this one. He said, "Well, it can't possibly be worse." And that really struck me. He's right, I thought. We were on the worst flight ever, but we were fine! And I realized in that moment that my fear of flying was gone. Poof!

2 **Retell the story to your partner as if a friend had told it to you. Use expressions for retelling a story in your conversation. Which story do you find more interesting? Why?**

PAIR WORK PRACTICE (STUDENT B)

7.4   EXERCISE 2C   STUDENT B

Read one perspective on the value of writing things by hand, and take notes.

In the age of computers and smartphones, why are we still asking schoolchildren to suffer through hours of painful penmanship lessons? Is handwriting really a life skill that is needed in the twenty-first century? In today's digital workplace, no one cares if your handwriting is neat, or even legible, because no one writes by hand anymore. Think about it. When did you last write out a full sentence?

Reports, memos, even shopping lists, are all tapped out on keyboards and keypads these days. It's far more important that children learn how to communicate effectively using the digital channels at their disposal than it is to impress their teacher with pretty penmanship.

12.3 EXERCISE 5A   STUDENT B

1   **Read a story about how life changed in an instant.**

Manny's story

My first year as a doctor was terrifying. There I was, an emergency room doctor but totally green and scared to death of doing something wrong. I had no confidence at all.

Then, this one night, the ER was understaffed, just one other doctor and me. Things were going OK – some minor injuries, and the flu was going around. But then we got word that there had been a big accident on the highway. Ambulances were on their way.

The next thing we knew, the ER was a madhouse – so many people with so many different injuries! I was standing there, frozen, when I felt a hand on my arm. I looked down and saw this old lady lying on a stretcher. She smiled at me and said, "Young man, do you know what the most comforting words in the world are?"

Shocked and confused, I finally sort of sputtered, "No, what?"

She pulled me closer and whispered, *"It's all right. I'm a doctor."*

I didn't get it at first, then it clicked. These people needed a doctor – a strong, decisive doctor. I nodded at her, took a deep breath, and got to work.

After that, everything changed. The ER became my home. And the first thing I do when a sick or injured person arrives is look them in the eye and say, "It's all right. I'm a doctor."

2   **Retell the story to your partner as if a friend had told it to you. Use expressions for retelling a story in your conversation. Which story do you find more interesting? Why?**

7.4   EXERCISE 2C   STUDENT C

Read one perspective on the value of writing things by hand, and take notes.

Have you ever noticed that hand-lettered motivational quotes fill the walls of trendy cafés, coffee shops, and hotel lobbies? A simple search online will confirm the current popularity of calligraphy – the art of drawing letters.

This love of lettering is becoming a popular hobby. Fans say that they enjoy the focus and discipline of this ancient art. There are long waiting lists for classes in trendy studios around the world – London, Wellington, Los Angeles. And online calligraphy tutorials are viewed by millions.

People are also making a living from the art, charging a high price for handwritten wedding invitations and promotional posters.

This page is intentionally left blank

This page is intentionally left blank

This page is intentionally left blank

This page is intentionally left blank

This page is intentionally left blank

This page is intentionally left blank

This page is intentionally left blank